T0149505

RIDIN'
THE GRUB LINE

LUCILLE M JENSEN

WESTBOW
PRESS®
A DIVISION OF THOMAS NELSON
& ZONDERVAN

WestBow Press books may be ordered through booksellers or by contacting:

WestBow Press
A Division of Thomas Nelson & Zondervan
1663 Liberty Drive
Bloomington, IN 47403
www.westbowpress.com
1 (866) 928-1240

ISBN: 978-1-5127-7886-1 (sc)
ISBN: 978-1-5127-7887-8 (hc)
ISBN: 978-1-5127-7885-4 (e)

Library of Congress Control Number: 2017903976

Print information available on the last page.

WestBow Press rev. date: 4/28/2017

Grandma and Grandpa Huestis and their five children
– The start of it all.

L-R: Fred & Achsah Crites, Cody & Florence Smith,
John & Marian Chvilicek, Frank & Ethel Smith, Flossie
& Francis Huestis, In Front: Francis & Alice Huestis

Four Generations: Ethel & Frank Smith, Francis & Alice
Huestis Dessie & Ralph Shipman & Ernest

L-R: Back Row: Frank, Grandpa H, Fred Crites, ?, George, ?, Charlie
and Ada Clemence, Ethel, Ralph, Marian, Lula, Frances, Flossie,
Mildred, Delilah, Dessie, Velma, Vera, Alice, Bernice. In front are
three Crites boys then Cleona Crites and Ora. I don't know who
the next boy is. I think -0the next three girls are Clemence girls
and I am the one in front of them. Reunion July 21, 1927

Dedication

I'm writing all this down for my kids and their kids and their kids and on down. I am 92 years old getting closer to 93. It has taken a long, long time to learn a lot of these things. Some, I wish I had learned as a child, but we lived nearly 20 miles from the nearest church, and we, as most people then, did not go that far by real horsepower for a one-hour service and then the 20 miles back. I don't remember and so never knew anything about God and Jesus except what Ora told me when I was 5, 6 or 7. I eventually learned after I turned to the Lord and accepted Him as my Savior that mother had always taught her children from the Bible. When she died, no one continued the practice. I don't remember having a Bible in the house. Lula, my second oldest sister, took over the household work after mother died. She gave me a Bible in the King James translation for 8th grade graduation. I was an avid reader but never managed to get past a couple of Old Testament chapters of the Bible. I wonder if it would have been different if I'd ever tried to read the New Testament. The most important parts of the Bible are the four Gospels: Matthew, Mark, Luke and John. The remaining books are more of a concordance to help you live the Christian life that the first four introduce. The Old Testament relates what had happened before and how God planned it all along. It tells how people mess up and how God can and will forgive, take them back and help them. It shows us the enormity of what is being done and who is doing it. We have a tendency to think the Bible is simply a list of do's and don'ts. It really explains God's plan for the world and how wonderful everything could be if we would just live His way. Then He explains what happens if we go against God's loving plans. It is so simple. God made us to walk upright on two feet. If we try to walk through a boulder, we trip, we fall and we hurt.

God isn't wreaking vengeance on us. We tried to go against a rule, and we found it hurt!

Epigraph

The old-time cowboys were hired on only for the summers. When winter came they were forced to fend for themselves and then they would travel from ranch to ranch staying and helping for a few days at a time wherever they happened to be. They called this "Ridin' the Grubline" since each ranch furnished food and shelter. I have tried to be accurate in my telling for the most part but I have to admit that my memory is not what it once was. So if you disagree with the way I have told it just mark it up to the vagaries of "old age".

ERRATA

Descendants of Lucille Mae Smith

Generation 1

1. **LUCILLE MAE SMITH** was born on 04 Apr 1924 in Farm north of Hingham, Hill County, Montana. She married HARRY THOMAS JENSEN on 25 Dec 1945 in Zion LutheranChurch, Glendive, Dawson Co, MT. He was born on 21 Feb 1920. He died on 06 May 2010.

Harry Thomas Jensen and Lucille (750652) Mae Smith had the following children:

   i.   MAE EVA JENSEN was born on 22 Dec 1946 in Glendive, Montana. She married JIMMIE DAVID RITTAL on 02 Sep 1967 in Circle, McCone, Montana, USA. He was born on 19 Dec 1941 in Circle, Montana.

   ii. TERRY SOREN JENSEN was born on 04 Dec 1948 in Glendive, Dawson, Montana, USA. He married BARBARA ELAINE SUKUT on 17 Dec 1969 in Glendive, Dawson, Montana, USA. She was born on 01 Nov 1949 in Glendive, Dawson, Montana, USA.

   iii. DEBRA ANN JENSEN was born on 29 Nov 1949 in Terry, Prairie, Montana, USA. She married DONALD ALLAN KLEPPELID on 17 Jun 1972 in Circle, McCone,

Montana, USA. He was born on 27 Dec 1951 in Circle, McCone, Montana, USA.

iv. DAVID THOMAS JENSEN was born on 06 Mar 1951 in Miles City, Custer, Montana, USA. He married MARY LYNN GEER on 09 Jun 1973 in Circle, McCone, Montana, USA. She was born on 29 Dec 1955 in Wolf Point, Roosevelt, Montana, USA.

GENERATION 2

2. **MAE EVA JENSEN** (Lucille Mae Smith) was born on 22 Dec 1946 in Glendive, Montana. She married JIMMIE DAVID RITTAL on 02 Sep 1967 in Circle, McCone, Montana, USA. He was born on 19 Dec 1941 in Circle, Montana.

Jimmie David Rittal and Mae Eva Jensen had the following children:

i. KAMI JO RITTAL was born on 24 Apr 1969 in Wolf Point, Roosevelt, Montana, USA. She married DOUGLAS ERIC YOST on 05 Jul 2002 in Sidney Rural, Richland, Montana, USA. He was born on 12 May 1971.

ii. KALI LYNN RITTAL was born on 04 Jul 1972 in Wolf Point, Roosevelt, Montana, USA. She married PAUL HAKJOONG KIM on 10 Sep 2005. He was born on 19 Jul 1967 in Seoul, Korea.

iii. HENRY LUKE RITTAL was born on 06 Aug 1976 in Sidney Rural, Richland, Montana, USA. He married ANN MARIE TOSCANO on 13 Mar 1999. She was born on 09 May 1976 in Danbury, Fairfield, Connecticut, USA.

iv. JOHN JIMMIE RITTAL (AKA071216) HANNA VALENTINA PRENTICE was born on 12 Jul 1981 in Sidney Rural, Richland, Montana, USA.

3. TERRY SOREN JENSEN (Lucille Mae Smith) was born on 04 Dec 1948 in Glendive, Dawson, Montana, USA. He married BARBARA ELAINE SUKUT on 17 Dec 1969 in Glendive, Dawson, Montana, USA. She was born on 01 Nov 1949 in Glendive, Dawson, Montana, USA.

Terry Soren Jensen and Barbara Elaine Sukut had the following children:

i. DANIEL3 ROWLAN was born in 1968 in Helena West, Lewis and Clark, Montana, USA. He married (1) DAWN MICHELLE JONES. She was born in 1968. He married (2) MANDI MARIE CHRISKE. She was born in 1975. He married (3) SHARLENE. She was born on 14 Apr 1970.

ii. JERRY THOMAS JENSEN was born on 26 Sep 1970 in Billings, Yellowstone, Montana, USA.

iii. TROY SOREN JENSEN was born on 18 Aug 1973 in Circle, McCone, Montana, USA. He married JANELLE LEE CURRY on 13 Sep 1997 in Sidney Rural, Richland, Montana, USA. She was born on 23 Oct 1970 in Miles City, Custer, Montana, USA.

4. DEBRA ANN JENSEN (Lucille Mae Smith) was born on 29 Nov 1949 in Terry, Prairie, Montana, USA. She married DONALD ALLAN KLEPPELID on 17 Jun 1972 in Circle, McCone,

Montana, USA. He was born on 27 Dec 1951 in Circle, McCone, Montana, USA.

Donald Allan Kleppelid and Debra Ann Jensen had the following children:

    i.   IAN BOSTON3 KLEPPELID was born on 09 Jun 1982 in Sidney Rural, Richland, Montana, USA. He married KAYLEE CHRISTINE LOVE on 15 Sep 2012 in Huntsville Rural, Walker, Texas, USA. She was born on 21 Jan 1987 in Huntsville Rural, Walker, Texas, USA.

    ii. DAMON THOMAS KLEPPELID was born on 16 Dec 1983 in Sidney Rural, Richland, Montana, USA. He married RILEY RENE' CHEATHAM on 02 May 2009 in Shepherd Hill Estates, Willis, TX. She was born on 26 Nov 1983 in Huntsville Rural, Walker, Texas, USA.

5. DAVID THOMAS JENSEN (Lucille Mae Smith) was born on 06 Mar 1951 in Miles City, Custer, Montana, USA. He married MARY LYNN GEER on 09 Jun 1973 in Circle, McCone, Montana, USA. She was born on 29 Dec 1955 in Wolf Point, Roosevelt, Montana, USA.

David Thomas Jensen and Mary Lynn Geer had the following children:

    i.   JOSHUA JON3 JENSEN was born on 18 May 1975 in Wolf Point, Roosevelt, Montana, USA. He married (1) JODEAN WORKMAN. She was born in 1976. He married (2) RENEE LEE MCLEAN on 04 Sep 2014 in Colstrip, Rosebud, Montana, USA. She was born on 11 Feb 1972 in Baltimore, Baltimore, Maryland, USA.

    ii. TRACIE ANN JENSEN was born on 27 Aug 1977 in Forsyth, Rosebud, Montana, USA. She married SCOTT

HUNTER ROTH on 29 Sep 2001. He was born on 30 Aug 1963 in Rapid City, Pennington, South Dakota, USA.

GENERATION 3

6. **KAMI JO RITTAL** (Mae Eva Jensen, Lucille Mae Smith) was born on 24 Apr 1969 in Wolf Point, Roosevelt, Montana, USA. She married DOUGLAS ERIC YOST on 05 Jul 2002 in Sidney Rural, Richland, Montana, USA. He was born on 12 May 1971.

Douglas Eric Yost and Kami Jo Rittal had the following children:

    i.   DARREL ALEXANDER YOST was born on 09 May 2005 in Holy Cross Hospital, Silver Springs, MD.

    ii.   DARBY ANN YOST was born on 07 Jul 2007 in Aberdeen, South Dakota.

    iii.   DARCY AVA YOST was born on 28 Jun 2011 in Aberdeen, South Dakota.

7. **KALI LYNN RITTAL** (Mae Eva Jensen, Lucille Mae Smith) was born on 04 Jul 1972 in Wolf Point, Roosevelt, Montana, USA. She married PAUL HAKJOONG KIM on 10 Sep 2005. He was born on 19 Jul 1967 in Seoul, Korea.

Paul Hakjoong Kim and Kali Lynn Rittal had the following children:

    i.   DAVID YOUNGKE4 KIM was born on 01 Dec 2006 in Los Angeles, California, USA.

    ii.   HENRY MINKI KIM was born on 21 Jun 2010 in Los Angeles, California, USA.

iii. MADELEINE CHAEWON KIM was born on 22 Feb 2013 in Encinitas, California.

8. **DANIEL ROWLAN** (Terry Soren Jensen, Lucille Mae Smith) was born in 1968 in Helena West, Lewis and Clark, Montana, USA. He married (1) DAWN MICHELLE JONES. She was born in 1968. He married (2) MANDI MARIE CHRISKE. She was born in 1975. He married (3) SHARLENE. She was born on 14 Apr 1970.

Daniel Rowlan and Dawn Michelle Jones had the following child:

i. CRYSTAL DAWN4 ROWLAN was born in 1992.

Daniel Rowlan and Mandi Marie Chriske had the following child:

ii. JULIA SAVANAH ROWLAN was born in 1996.

9. **TROY SOREN JENSEN** (Terry Soren, Lucille Mae Smith) was born on 18 Aug 1973 in Circle, McCone, Montana, USA. He married JANELLE LEE CURRY on 13 Sep 1997 in Sidney Rural, Richland, Montana, USA. She was born on 23 Oct 1970 in Miles City, Custer, Montana, USA.

Troy Soren Jensen and Janelle Lee Curry had the following children:

i. JORY (JENSEN)4 BRIGHT was born on 24 Dec 1992.

ii. EVERETT LEE JENSEN was born on 19 Oct 2001 in Sidney Rural, Richland, Montana, USA.

10. **DAMON THOMAS KLEPPELID** (Debra Ann Jensen, Lucille Mae Smith) was born on 16 Dec 1983 in Sidney Rural, Richland, Montana, USA. He married RILEY RENE' CHEATHAM on 02

May 2009 in Shepherd Hill Estates, Willis, TX. She was born on 26 Nov 1983 in Huntsville Rural, Walker, Texas, USA

Damon Thomas Kleppelid and Riley Rene' Cheatham had the following child:

i. LILLIAN MAXINE4 KLEPPELID was born on 17 May 2011 in Huntsville Rural, Walker, Texas, USA.

11. **JOSHUA JON JENSEN** (David Thomas, Lucille Mae Smith) was born on 18 May 1975 in Wolf Point, Roosevelt, Montana, USA. He married (1) JODEAN WORKMAN. She was born in 1976. He married (2) RENEE LEE MCLEAN on 04 Sep 2014 in Colstrip, Rosebud, Montana, USA. She was born on 11 Feb 1972 in Baltimore, Baltimore, Maryland, USA.

Joshua Jon Jensen and Jodean Workman had the following child:

i. JARROD JON4 JENSEN was born on 15 Mar 1993 in Billings, Yellowstone, Montana, USA.

Joshua Jon Jensen and Renee Lee McLean had the following children:

ii. SHANE DAVID JENSEN was born on 10 Feb 2012 in Billings, Yellowstone, Montana, USA.

iii. AARON DAKOTA KEPLIN was born on 27 Jul 1996 in Bismarck, Burleigh, North Dakota, USA.

iv. MEPHIS ISIAH KEPLIN was born on 01 May 2002 in Billings, Yellowstone, Montana, USA.

12. **TRACIE ANN JENSEN** (David Thomas, Lucille Mae Smith) was born on 27 Aug 1977 in Forsyth, Rosebud, Montana, USA. She

married SCOTT HUNTER ROTH on 29 Sep 2001. He was born on 30 Aug 1963 in Rapid City, Pennington, South Dakota, USA.

Scott Hunter Roth and Tracie Ann Jensen had the following children:

i. JACOB HUNTER4 ROTH was born on 31 May 2003 in Spearfish, Lawrence, South Dakota, USA.

ii. ALISON MARY ROTH was born on 15 Jul 2004 in Spearfish, Lawrence, South Dakota, USA.

iii. MEGAN ANN ROTH was born on 13 Jun 2008 in Rapid City, Pennington, South Dakota, USA.

GENERATION 4

13. JORY (JENSEN) BRIGHT (Troy Soren Jensen, Terry Soren Jensen, Lucille Mae Smith) was born on 24 Dec 1992.

Jory (Jensen) Bright had the following child:

i. MAYCEE (BRIGHT) HUGHES was born on 26 Oct 2014.

God has invited humans to join with him in what he himself called "very good." He called all other creation "good," but after He created the man and woman, He called it "very good," and it is in this that He has called people to join Him. With the animals, He spoke the word, and they were there complete. With mankind, He created them and then breathed life (spirit-soul) into them. And this is the role He plays at every conception. If He weren't there at every conception, there would be no soul for the new human, but because He is there, we now have a being with a soul. God is always there. "Never will I leave you, never will I forsake you." (Heb 13:5 NIV). Both man and woman should enjoy this feeling of exaltation when creating a new life. It should be an equal joy, and the man has the greatest responsibility in accomplishing this joy. The couple needs to realize the enormity of what they are doing and who is with them. Never confuse "exalt" which means dignify, honor, praise, glorify, magnify and uplift with the similar word "exult" which can feel much the same in some ways but really means vaunt, gloat, boast, or crow. The sounds are very close, but exult is definitely all human, while exalt contains God's presence and influence, the Glory of creating a new Baby!!!

Frank and Ethel Smith's first 5 children beside their sod house

Lucille Smith - 9 mos.
Standing on a chair

Lucille (LukieTeal) Smith

Floyd Smith

My oldest sister, Dessie, married Ralph Shipman, and had a son, Ernie, who was a year older than our youngest brother, Floyd. After they were grown, Ernie enjoyed letting everyone know that Floyd was his "old" Uncle. Dessie died when Ernie was a little over a year old, and not long after Mother passed. With Mother and Dessie gone, Ernie's Grandmother Shipman took over caring for Ernie and Lula took care of Floyd, Ora and I and of course all the housekeeping in our home. Our sister, Vera, who was next after Velma, died of Spinal meningitis around this time too, and was about 11 or 12. I just barely remember her as a beautiful blonde-haired girl with long blonde curls. Grandpa Huestis died sometime about then, too. I don't remember him at all. Both of my dad's parents were dead before I was born. When I was a freshman in high school, my sister, Velma, died, leaving her husband, Alfred Johnson and baby, Marlene, behind. I remember that Alfred asked our four brothers to be pallbearers at Velma's funeral. I don't remember who the other two were.

One especially heart-wrenching funeral was nephew, Harold Connor, Alice's baby. Alice was baking bread that day, and after taking the last loaf from the oven of the old coal/wood stove, she had allowed the fire to die down, relaxed and put baby Hal to bed for his nap. She started planning supper and because even in towns a refrigerator was a definite luxury all fresh foods needed to be replenished about daily. Alice decided while Hal was sleeping, she'd go the short walk to the store and get the needed fresh meat for supper. In the 15 to 20 minutes it took her to get it and start home again, the house was engulfed in flames. The fireman got the fire out, but the baby suffocated. Alice tried to go into the fire to get him, but the neighbors held her back as she was already several months along with Lyle, their second child. It was too late. The fire had started in the chimney and spread so far before it was ever noticed. How it could burn like that in a small town without being spotted is just unbelievable. That was the time of day for kids to be playing on the streets, mothers, like Alice, doing their last minute shopping, friends heading home from afternoon visits. Altogether it was probably the busiest time of the day. And still no one saw it.

Hal (Harold) son of Alice & Lavern Connor 1936

Dessie and Lula Smith 8/20/1926

Lula and Lucille

Mother was 16 when she married Dad, and she was 42 when she died. The pictures we have of her as a young girl show a beautiful young woman. Dad was 32 when they married. Wouldn't that cause a furor now days! Harry's dad was 32 and his mother 16 when they married, too. It was very common then. In fact, Harry's cousin, Buelah, was a grandmother at 32. Mother miscarried her fourteenth child and because of that, she began to bleed, and the bleeding would not stop. It still couldn't be stopped at the hospital in Havre, so that was where she died. She was terribly over weight and doctors today say she was very likely diabetic. It was before the time of treatment with insulin and also before any one did transfusions for loss of blood. Maybe a c-section would have saved her. I don't know. I know diabetics still have trouble carrying children.

Orrie Ethel Huestis Smith –
15 yrs. – Always called Ethel

Francis (Frank) Adelbert Smith
- 32 yrs. Cir. 1902

Ethel Smith

Frank A Smith

Ora, Floyd and Lucille

Alice with Dude and Doris.

Velma Smith Johnson

Lucille & Floyd

I was maybe 5 years old and Floyd was one, and Ora seven. Lee was 24, George was 21, Howard was 20, Lula was18, Alice was 16, and Velma 14 at the time of Mother's death. Between the time Velma and Ora were born there were three others, girls, Vera was born in 1917 and the twin girls, Lena and Leona were born and also died in 1920. I was number 12 in a family of 13. Numbers 7 and 8 were the twins, Lena and Leona, but they died before they were a year old. I think they died during the flu epidemic of WW1. All the rest of the family was comparatively healthy until Mother's 14th pregnancy. It ended in the miscarriage and extreme bleeding that couldn't be controlled.

Most years, the whole clan gathered to celebrate the holidays. They were Fourth of July, Thanksgiving, and Christmas. No gifts were ever exchanged. There was only one year when Dad came home with a doll a piece for my sister, Ora, and me and a truck for my brother, Floyd. My doll never lasted through its first family gathering. My one 10-cent ring was too small for my ring finger and so loose on my little finger that it only lasted about 1 week. None of these things were ever replaced. When something was gone, it was gone. I don't remember anyone saying we couldn't afford something we asked for. We just never asked. There was a pencil box that I saw in a sale catalog. It had a ruler, an eraser, maybe a pen and a couple pencils. Each item had its own little compartment, and I pictured it in all bright colors even though all catalogs were black and white. I wanted it so bad but never asked for it because it cost seventeen cents!

Grandma Huestis and daughters Achsah and Ethel with their families

Until I was nine, the house we lived in was located on a small hill, so the driveway sloped away from the house. This made it perfect for some of the entertainment we had.

I remember the fun we had walking barrels. We started with an empty 55 gallon oil steel drum and laid it on its side. Next, one rider at a time balanced upright on the middle top of the barrel and walked backwards making the barrel roll forward down the hill. It was touchy. There was a fine line between being in control as you went down-hill or losing control when the barrel gained speed and dumped its rider. There were many bruises and minor cuts and scrapes, but I don't remember adults telling us to stop "because you'll get hurt." We learned the hard way and either learned to do it better or not do it at all!!

Another game we liked was getting inside a barrel with one end open. Another kid would give the barrel a push at the top of the hill, and it gained speed as it rolled all the way to the bottom. Rough! Bruises and hurts, but "fun!"

The barn was built with a tall center section for hay storage. The animal stalls were in lean-tos on each side of the center. The lean-tos were approximately 6 ft. high on the outside, going up to the eaves of the central part. The attached side was only a couple feet below the eaves of the tall center. With a pile of hay on the low side, we had a perfect access to the high slope of the center roof. To make it even better there were no shingles on the roof and the boards started at the peak and made a perfect slide. If we did it just right, we slid all the way down to the hay by squatting on our haunches with our feet under us. I had one little problem. I got off balance and slid all the way down on my bottom. On the way, I picked up a sliver about an inch long and about the size of a large darning needle. It went deep!! At first some of it showed. Lula tried everything they knew to get it out. She used tweezers to pull it out, but it broke off, so she used a sterilized needle to get it, but that didn't work. After several days, it festered, and she tried to squeeze it out. When it still didn't move, the next method was filling a beer bottle with boiling water. After letting it set for a short time, she emptied the bottle and placed the open end of the hot bottle over the spot where the sliver went in. By holding it in place as it cooled, a suction was created that was supposed to draw the sliver out. None of this worked, so the sliver stayed. All these years, I have been able to feel the bump until just a couple-three years ago. Apparently it has finally dissolved!

We made our own stilts so they could be any height we wanted---or had nerve to go. I think 2 or 3 feet was about as high as we dared.

The older kids had stories about times Mom and Dad would take the younger kids with them to go visiting, and the older ones---- Lee, Dessie, George, Howard, Lula, and Alice---- stayed home. One way they liked to entertain themselves while home alone was to catch and saddle the horse that was kept in the corral, and use it to crowd a herd of wild horses off the range into the corral and on into the barn. They squeezed as many in as would fit. Then they went inside the barn and walked across the backs of those wild broncs from one end of the barn to the other. I positively cannot understand how they all lived through it. If that got boring, they could try what was definitely a "no, no." They'd herd a bunch of the cattle into the corral and have impromptu rodeos. These animals were the ones that were to be sold and did not need the "fat run off them." It was still fun and went off with no drastic consequences, except once when Howard managed to get a shoulder pulled out of joint during one of his rides. What to do? Can't call a doctor. Can't have Dad find out. Lee proudly saved the day. He took hold of the damaged arm, put one foot in Howard's armpit and pulled until the joint popped back into place. The folks never knew a thing about it.

In the winter, when the evenings got long, we passed the time doing all kinds of exercises---- walk under the broomstick, climb through the broomstick, jump over it. We'd stand on our heads against the wall and try to hand walk away from it. We'd try to drink water while standing on our heads. Another one was to stand up straight and put your hands over your head, then start leaning back like a back bend until you touched the floor behind your feet. As we got better, we could lay our hands on the floor in back of our feet and bend until they were in front of our feet. We were all taller than most of our friends, and Dad told us to stand straight and tall like a young pine. I always remember Mother as being short until Alice told me that she and Mother were the same height.

Lula always called her "my mother," even when talking to the rest of us. Ora always talked of "my father" in the same way. The rest of us always just said Mother or Father except when we were talking to people outside the family.

We all learned to play card games--- Old Maid, War, hearts, rummy and lots of others that I can't remember the names. Eventually, as we got older, we learned the grown-up games like whist and pinochle. We played poker with matches instead of money. These were the matches that could be lit by scratching along any rough surface, yet we were taught about the danger and how to use them safely and to carefully put them back in the boxes when we finished playing, The cards were used until they were completely worn out. If they got sticky, we just spread them out on the table, sprinkled a little talcum, starch or baby powder on them, swished them around for a while then picked them out of the powder, and they were ready for another game. New decks came with an extra card or two plus the jokers. Since the jokers were seldom needed in the games we played, they were always available for replacing any no longer usable card. We would mark the joker with the suit and the number of the missing card. Of course, the jokers were so new and clean that they stuck out like a sore thumb for a while. The old cards had to be in pretty bad shape to get replaced.

Ora and I played a game we made up with the Atlas. One of us opened the Atlas to a state map. The one holding the atlas covered the name, and the other had to identify the state by the rest of the information on the page. We learned all the states, their capitols as well as their rivers, large cities and any other info the atlas had in it. And we were having fun.

Floyd on Paint taken near Polson, Montana

Alice & Vera on Maud

When mother died, we were living just a mile west of the Mariner schoolhouse. Anna Dolezal and her family lived---- I think---- a mile south of us. Sometimes their school kids walked past our place on the way to school; at other times, they took a cut across through our pasture. The older three girls---- Lula, Alice and Velma--- batched (lived alone, without our parents) in Hingham in a rented house during the school terms. Ora and I stayed with them the year I was in the third grade. It was also the year I had pink eye. It was so bad my eyes were glued shut every morning. The girls would use warm water to wash them open. I spent my time in bed with the shades down, so I guess that's what saved my eyes. I remember, one evening that I watched the older three girls all getting ready to go to a dance. I was only able to open my eyes about halfway. The nearest high school was in the town of Hingham, and they were all in high school. Alice, Velma and Lula were on the girls basketball team the year Hingham won Hi-line championship. Those girls were also the track champions in the 1930-31 school year.

Lula – 3rd from Left and Alice is Fifth from Left

Back row – Velma 4th from Left
Alice is fifth from Left – front row

This story is definitely not chronological!! Back to the Mariner School for a couple more memories.

At Mariner school, my best friend was Gudrun Kapperud. She was in my class. Another was my cousin, Frank Huestis. He was so smart and knew all of the arithmetic answers while it was all Dutch to me. Leif Kapperud, Gudrun's brother, was, I believe, an 8th grader and the oldest in his family, so he was responsible for the care of the horses they used. One noon that winter, when he went to care for the horses, one of them kicked him in the thigh and broke it. He had to be taken by sleigh to the doctor to get it set. I have no idea where the doctor was, but I think it was most likely Havre, which was 50 or 60 miles away.

One spring day the Dolezal kids and we were walking to school. I got stuck in the mud and lost one overshoe in a low, wet spot in the road. George Dolezal came to my rescue. He lifted me and my over-shoe up and carried me to high ground where he helped me put my over-shoe back on so we could all go on to school. It is odd how memory works. I don't remember anymore about him or the rest of the family except that was about the time jigsaw puzzles came out. The whole Dolezal family came to visit us with a puzzle, and we all went to work and put it together. Their baby, Jackie, was just at the crawling age. They said whenever a piece couldn't be found "Jackie took it." He was too young to defend himself. I know they moved to a ranch in the Sweet Grass Hills sometime later.

I tried taking typing in high school, and I just absolutely could not do it. So I just quit going to class instead of dropping it and making it official. So, of course, that counted as a failing class. But in all the others, I got good enough grades that I still ended up as the salutatorian in my class. School was easy for me. I had always hated arithmetic, but I loved algebra and geometry because there was reasoning to it, and I could easily figure it out. When my niece, Marli and daughter, Debbie had trouble with their geometry, they brought it to me, and I helped them learn the basics. After that they had no problems. Their teacher was a genius who could know the answer but couldn't explain how he arrived at the answer.

In my high-school history class, we had a weekly newspaper. Every time the paper came, we read it and then the teacher gave us a test on it. He got the bright idea that the student who got the highest score on the test, had to make up the test for the next week. So one week I wrote the test, then the next week Jerry Hovland wrote it. We went through the whole year taking turns getting the highest grade and writing the test.

Lucille M Smith – school outfit that I sewed.
At Campus Clean Up

Building a hay wagon and everyone worked when needed.

The Fairchild School was all that was left of Fairchild, one of the hundreds of small towns that dotted the prairies in the homestead days. They usually had a general store and post office in one building. I'm sure they had at least one bar, perhaps a livery stable and/or blacksmith shop and a school, maybe a church. Shortly after we went to school there, that school, too, was abandoned. Eventually the building was sold, and the new owners remodeled it into a home. Absolutely nothing remains at the location where we had lived; no house, no barn, no fences, not even the dam and small reservoir Dad made with team and "slip." Remember the old saying, "you can't go home."? My "old home" is one solid stretch of wheat waving in the summer breeze.

My old home once stood in the middle of what is now a wheat field.

I stopped in Butte on my way to the coast and visited with Ed and Delilah Huestis Tangmo. I don't know if I planned to stay long, but they needed a waitress at the combination Greyhound Bus Station/ Restaurant, so I went to work there. I remember it as a filthy, dirty place, but if you wanted to use the buses, it was the only place. Anyway, I got put on the swing shift working from 4 p.m. to 12 midnight. It was during my first and only swing shift at that café when a soldier got off the bus. He was excited about getting home and seeing his girlfriend who worked there, but she was not excited about seeing him. She used her job as her excuse, and he was determined to see her as she left work at midnight, so he sat the whole shift feeding nickles, (yes, nickles could feed a jukebox back then) into the jukebox and played one, and only one song. I remember only a few of the words to the song he played. Poor guy, we sympathized with him at first. But after hearing, "Have I stayed away too long," then something about, "will you still be my darlin' or have I stayed away too long?" over and over and over, we lost all sense of sympathy! The people who were able to get on a bus and leave were the lucky ones. The waitress grew less popular as people grew more and more sick of hearing that song. Anyone unable to leave debated using an ax on it or at least unplugging the blasted thing, and they all sympathized with the soldier.

My shift ended, and I had to walk home. I was thankful to be leaving that song behind me. The next morning when Ed and Delilah realized I had walked home in Butte, "in a dark part of Butte, and all alone," they told me, "No way will you work there anymore." They were horrified that the manager hadn't made arrangements for me to ride home instead of letting me "Walk home in Butte at night!" I never did go back and had no idea of how the story ended, but the song still pops into my head with amazing regularity, and it is over seventy years now.

You know, as I look back, I can see this is just one of the times that the Lord took care of me and protected me. I was SO naive and trusting that it was pitiful. When I was working at the shipyard in Vancouver, Washington, I invited one of the crew to my apartment for supper, and that's all there was to it. He left right after eating. The next day, my girlfriend told me that he was a married man. I was so angry at myself for "dating" a "married man." I was completely horrified at myself so much that I cried all day as I welded. I think Gen cussed him out, and he came and apologized saying, "I'll never tell anyone."

My answer, "I'll always know I dated a married man." I didn't care if anyone else knew or not! I've thought since then, "Of course you won't tell anyone. They might tell your wife."

Then there was the time another friend arranged double dates for us to go for a ride on the river in a rented boat. We scarcely got started when the other couple went below. We couldn't even look at each other we were so embarrassed.

When my girlfriend's fiance came home on leave, they stopped at my apartment before work. They left me with a water glass full of whiskey and orders to drink it before I went to work because I couldn't go to celebrate with them! I did! I can't understand how I lived through it. I was very happy (?) all shift, skinned my shin clear to the bone, never even covered it with a bandage. I don't remember even getting a headache, and the skin healed fast! Brother!! I was so dumb. And I was 20 years old!!!!

It is never a "one-night-stand." The after effects are too, too far-reaching every time; not always immediately as in a pregnancy, but, like modern medicine, there can be "side effects." Some maybe soon, but some may lie hidden for years. A one-night-stand: a short period of time in the life of two people when they do whatever, including sex, for a couple of hours, then each goes his/her way with no repercussions, no liability, no ties, no responsibilities.

In other words, it is a completely false picture ---a delusion that always has its results. Some results show up immediately with feelings of guilt and shame. Then there are always the follow ups that can come at any time in life. There are so many consequences, so many possibilities.

There is only one sure, 100% sure, way to prevent the unwanted results. Abstinence. And this goes for both parties. How many men do you know who find out later that the "one-night- stand" is still living on and wants to meet his/her "real" father. And if you finally hear about and meet one----what if there are others you don't know about? What if a legitimate and an illegitimate one meet and feel attracted to each other and want to marry? A one-night-stand has lasted 25 years, plus or minus. The children who result from this 'one night stand' are the main ones who suffer. They go throughout their lives suffering in one way or another. They put on a show and few people see it, but those who really know them find that they continue to have deeply embedded issues related to it.

Modern day has turned something that is holy and private, (creating a new human-being), into something dirty, clandestine, and shameful.

I was in the 5th grade in the Fairchild School when I finally learned to read for fun. In the middle of my history lesson, the words all at once became sentences, and the sentences became stories. That was the beginning of my addiction. There were always new magazines at our home, but they were not enough to keep me busy. I read every book in each school library and even resorted to encyclopedias and dictionaries when desperate. Books were precious.

Never write in a book!

Never fold the corner of a page!

Never break the spine by bending the book too far open!

These rules came from Dad who still had his 5th-grade reader with its cloth cover. The cloth was from the leftover fabric his mother had used to make a dress. He gave his Reader to me since I was such an avid reader. I have cherished it all these years and passed it on to my oldest son. I hope it will continue to be cherished and passed on through the family who love books. They are becoming rare and treated casually if at all.

We went to the Fairchild school one day ---Ora, Floyd and I. At the ringing of the bell, all students went to their desks and found a blank sheet of paper on the desk. Mr Sterry(Alton) told everyone not to touch the paper yet. "You will have a timed snap quiz. I will time you, so are you ready?" We all grabbed our pencils (no ball point pens then). He looked at his watch, waited a while, then said, "Go!" We rushed to turn the page and found two words that filled the entire page---

APRIL'S
FOOL

Joy, peace, pain, love, hurt, satisfaction, worry, happiness, work, help, sadness, kindness, grief, mourning, blessing,---- in other words living. It isn't "making love," "screwing," f------", "cuddling," "having a piece of tail," or any of the other nasty expressions for the most holy act known to mankind: "Creating a new human."

In this act between a married man and woman, God is there making something that is impossible into something possible.

They are creating a new human. (See Genesis 4:1 NIV).

This is the true intent of this action. This is the correct attitude for both participants. It is a serious holy contract each is entering with God and his/her spouse. They are making a promise to God concerning this new human's whole life.

Ora used to get mad at me, and she'd start beating on me, and I'd run. I can remember running around and around the house 'till finally the day came when I got mad, and I turned on her and started beating on her. I always had long fingernails. She chewed her nails; I didn't. I turned on her, started scratching her and beating on her and got the best of her. She was a little more careful after that about how she'd get mad at me and start chasing me. I don't remember at all why she got mad, but she could get mad pretty easily. Anyway, when she showed the scratches to Lula--- this was after Mother had died, and Lula was taking Mother's place, Lula trimmed my fingernails down to the quick. I bawled and bawled and bawled.

I liked my long fingernails. I didn't use them for scratching people after that anyway.

I was 9 years old when we moved to land north of Gildford. There were no buildings on the place, so we built them. We put up the studs for a wall, then covered both the inside and outside with boards. Before the roof was added we stirred up a sort of Adobe mix. Each wall section was filled with this filler made of mud and straw so it was warm in winter and cool in summer. The inside walls were covered with that blue building paper and painted with Kalsomine, a tinted whitewash. Maybe that's when I decided I didn't like anything blue except the Montana skies. The pasture land bordered the Milk River, and we were near the Canadian border.

L to R: Lucille & Harry Jensen, Ora & Monte Hewitt,
Lavern Connor beside the Milk River

We were living very close to the Milk River as shown in this picture. There is a grave on the north side of this stretch of the river. It is where a couple buried their baby. They thought they were in the U.S. But when the survey came through they discovered they were in Canada. I don't remember if they moved the remains to the U.S. side or not.

While the men were working along the river bottom, Ora and I decided to see the view from above. It was, of course, fabulous. As we started back down, it turned into a race. It really isn't very smart to run downhill---especially a very steep hill, practically a cut-bank. I managed to stay on my feet, but poor Ora tripped or slipped and landed full length into a huge collection of Russian thistles. Ouch!

The flies were horrible. We had no screens on the windows or doors. We had to open all windows and doors for ventilation. I can remember taking dish towels and two or three of us would start on the back wall of the far room and chase the flies into the next room. Then we shut that door and started on that room. When we got as many as possible all together, we sprayed them with the fly spray, Flit or one of the many other brands. One problem, the fly spray didn't kill them. It only stunned them so we only had about 15 minutes to let the air clear so that we could breath it before we had to have the stunned flies swept up and dropped in the hot stove to burn. Yuk! Horrible job!

Hand pumped sprayer for insect spray

YOU WORSHIP YOUR GOD, I'LL WORSHIP MINE

There's only one problem with this idea, and it is a big one---- there is only ONE God who is the true God. So when you "worship your god," what exactly is happening? Well, you are doing several things----saying, "I can do as I please with no repercussions." In that, we say God has no power over us. We say He is powerless. We are telling Him His Word is nonsense, and because we aren't wise enough to recognize our own inadequacy, we say, "See, I am doing just fine without You." We don't recognize His great love for us by the way He gives us the chance to change. He has arranged for our salvation to be so easily achieved in such a short time with so little effort on our part. When the day comes, and it <u>will</u> come, that we will realize how very wrong we have been, it will only take a split second for an appeal to go to God (He's been right at our side waiting for this moment). So in your distress, you may only have time to say, "Please, God," or, "Yes, Jesus," but that is enough. He just opens His arms and answers, "Yes." Then we awake in His presence or to the rest of our life with Him. Then we can begin to live a life of greater joy than we had ever dreamed possible here on earth.

That joy is not happiness; it's not gladness. It is a joy that it is almost beyond description. It doesn't depend on money, fancy clothes, expensive things, houses, cars, people, location, weather, or the many things that are seen. It is a deep, deep comfort, resting, believing, depending, love overflowing, that we can just feel and know it is there, no matter where we are or what our surroundings are telling us. If we aren't careful, we can find ourselves worshipping Satan or one of his demons. Now is especially the time to study God's Word. He gave us His Word to help us and guide us. Don't think this means you will never have another problem in your life. He never promised no problems, but He will be there to help us through it all. We will have His strength and love bearing us through these problems, and we will be the conquerors in the end. When we turn to God, it makes Satan have a hissy fit, and he'll do anything he can think of to make us believe we made the wrong decision. Satan is a rotten, sneaky, lying thief, and coward but he shows himself to look good. He is the original con man/woman. He can show himself as both. He is also cruel. Any kindness or caring from Satan is a façade, but he's patient---- waiting and waiting. He's also strong. Possessed people can have great physical strength. Through all this, there is One who is stronger, more loving, more patient, more caring, completely honest, filled with truth. Of course, He is our loving God/ Jesus. Satan becomes impotent when we stay beside Jesus.

Jesus is the source of our power.

I've always read everything I could lay my hands on and think that is what made school so easy. I also memorized a lot. My family started that when I was a child learning to talk, they taught me nursery rhymes and other poetry. I've forgotten much of it since my brain infection. That was a truly horrifying time to me. I pray that I <u>never, never</u> have hallucinations again. I think if I'd had someone to keep reassuring me that it was all caused by the meds, it would have helped. I needed reassurance over and over. Only when I turned to my Bible did the horror go away. So that was another time the Lord protected me.

Dad bought a brand new Singer sewing machine and brought it home for Mother. I don't know exactly what year this was, but it was after I was born and before Floyd. After Mother died, Lula was the one who did the sewing. Alice and Velma may have done some, too, but by the time I remember, Lula was the only one of the three older girls still home.

Before school started in the fall, Lula would sit down with the Sears Roebuck or Montgomery Ward catalog, and we were allowed to choose the yard goods for our new school dresses, one each, I think. The fabric we could afford was $0.10 a yard. Even I, at that age, could see the poor quality because it was thin and loosely woven.

We also wore long stockings and "bloomers," plus long johns in winter!! Lula sewed the dresses and bloomers: loose fitting knee-length under panties with an elastic waist and elastic at the leg openings at the knees. Some of our bloomers were made from flour sacks or feed sacks. We rolled elastic garters into the tops of the long cotton stockings to hold them up.

The only time I willingly did my share of dish washing was when Lula said, "I'll start on your dress if you will get the dishes done."

"Love" itself has been reinterpreted over the years. The English language falls short when it talks about love. God's Word has three kinds of love and a name for each. Americans have used the word "love" when they should be using still others. Love has been stretched to the breaking point. It is used to cover way too many things from admiration of an unusual pebble to devoted feelings for a life partner. The correct definition for love is well stated in the Bible (John 21:15 -19 RSV). Jesus used two of the different words, but translations of the Bible use only one word, "love," while each has a different meaning.

The three kinds of love are ideally found in families. To start it all there is the friendship sort. Children feel this for siblings, cousins, and others outside their immediate family. Then there is the love that children receive from their parents. This is more of a creative feeling where one builds (trains, molds, shapes), the baby to build a successful adult. The third one is the love a person has for one of the opposite sex. This has to be a combination of the first two, plus the sexual attraction. Both need to have all three forms of love for their mate. A persons' whole life is a growing, shaping, building process.

Ideally, both parties come to the marriage as virgins, ready for the miracle of joining God in the creation of another human being. They come with clean healthy bodies. Neither one needs to fear disease or filth of any kind. It can and should be a time of mutual love, caring, exploration, joy, tenderness, truth, gentleness, and openness. A time of experimentation, getting truly acquainted, learning likes and dislikes and how to accommodate to one another with <u>no one</u> else around---- always with love.

We always had a good crop of rhubarb, so even though "we didn't like it," we always ate it, especially rhubarb sauce. Mainly because there was no other fruit on hand.

Mom baked all of our bread, of course. On one day each week, she baked a week's supply. There was always enough dough to also make a couple of pans of her cinnamon rolls with her own recipe. If there was no old bread left for dinner (which is noon) on baking day, we ate fried bread. It was always fried on demand so we could melt the butter on the really hot bread. Everything was served hot off the stove. Cold food was a serious no-no!

The best hotcakes went straight from the griddle to someone's own plate without a stop at a platter. The same went for the bread. The first loaf out of the oven was always passed around---- scorching hot, and we tore off the part we liked. I always went for the nice crunchy crust with lots of homemade sweet butter and maybe sometime sugar and cinnamon. I remember one of the pans Mother used for baking bread held five loaves.

Bedtime snacks--- bread with sour cream and sugar, or a cup of milk with bread and raisins dropped in the milk. If we wanted something a little bit special, we could use saltine crackers instead of bread. There was always a container of good thick sour cream to spread on the bread with sugar, too. We often ate cukes, carrots and peas straight from the garden. My idea of a perfect meal consists of a green vegetable salad with medium rare beef-steak. We made sandwiches with homemade bread and butter and radishes. We never ate raw green beans like we did the other veggies. When my oldest grandson got old enough to "help" in the garden, he ate the green beans directly from the vines, and our Vietnamese friends just loved raw corn on the cob. I was dumbfounded, so I tried them, too, and found they were good. I wonder why none of us had ever eaten them before as we really liked so many other raw vegetables.

When the cousins came over during early rhubarb season, about the first thing we kids did was grab the salt shaker and go to the rhubarb patch. Nothing was so good as biting into a fresh picked stalk of nice crunchy salty rhubarb unless it was that rhubarb sauce with a slice of homemade bread and butter.

Casual sex-this is definitely a misnomer. There can never be 'casual sex'. That act in itself is a cause for so many effects when sex is treated casually. It turns into a few minutes of fun for them, and it becomes a "wham bam, thank you, ma'am" and the man goes on his merry way. For a woman, it soon becomes a matter of, "well he certainly didn't satisfy me, oh well, maybe the next time will be better." Of course they practice "safe" sex, and if by some far-off unlikely chance, a safeguard should fail, they can always kill the little bastard. Although it is prettied up by calling it "having an abortion". "It's perfectly legal you know." Legal doesn't always equal right or correct. And because God is always with each and every person, there is no way it can be hidden.

When raising children, all need the same for the first 5 years. When they err, punish them, then forget it. Don't bring it up and tell everyone about the naughty thing he or she did. The child sees it as a way to get attention. No one ever stops wanting attention. If you want a well-behaved loving child, you must set the example of such an adult. Every boy wants to grow up like Daddy and every girl wants to become like Mama --- at least for the first five years of their lives, and those are the foundation years. We must look at ourselves and ask ourselves "Am I being the kind of person I want my child to become?"

Love them, hug them, tell them, show them, and tell others about the good they do.

If a toddler reaches for something dangerous, it's perfectly all right to slap that little hand and say, "Don't do that, honey, it will hurt you." The hurt will be connected to the dangerous item, not to you, so you are still seen as someone who is loving and caring, and the dangerous item is to be avoided. You must be consistent and patient.

Remember that there is a difference between discomfort and hurt. The slap on the hand is discomfort. What would happen without the restraining slap is hurt. The importance of those first five years can never be overemphasized. They are the strong foundation set for a long happy life of a happy useful caring person. Or they can be crumbling but equally strong in another sense, foundation for a sad, unhappy, selfish, cruel person. The main way parents teach in these young years is by example. At this age, learning seems to be a product of osmosis. They don't seem to hear it or feel it or see it, but by some God-given magical process, they absorb it, and they are not to be fooled. I feel that this is why, if at all possible, mothers should stay home with children under five.

Call it "Fun," but it is really an exultation. Far, far above "mere fun." Males know only this joy derived from the very act, but females know the deep long-lasting joy of continued sharing with God in the development of that new human being. The poor male has to live with caring for two people now and only one that he can see. It is his time of submission, and it is especially hard for male egos at this time. Only real men can successfully adapt to this new role. He is no longer alone in the center of his wife's life. He must learn to share his position as he enters his new baby into his own already busy center. He can't see it, or touch it. He has to have faith that it is there and will change him and his wife from a couple to completeness, a family. There will be a growing awareness of the immensity of the great responsibilities they have undertaken, but when the baby begins making its presence known, the great love and joy that gives him the strength to carry on, also grows.

Canning 1   Canning 2

To can rhubarb, we picked and washed it, trimmed the ends, and then cut it into half-inch pieces, put the rhubarb pieces into the jar --- filled the jar full---- then pumped water, fresh out of the well into the jar up to the very top so there was no room for air, and put the lid on and tightened it down. That rhubarb would taste just like fresh all winter long. It was just amazing how it kept. I look back and marvel.

The summer before my senior year in high school, I did all that canning myself. I was 16 years old. Somewhere I have pictures of the stuff I canned. Lula and Ken didn't live there anymore. They had their own place, so there was Howard, Floyd, Dad and myself. Ora had gone out to the coast, and she was living in Seattle and worked for Boeing as a "Rosie the Rive ter", building bombers and other aircraft necessary for the war effort.

It is very important, too, to be careful what you watch, what you read, and what you let your children watch and read. To let children watch horrible, cruel movies is going into partnership with Satan. He's going to attack your children often enough. He doesn't need your cooperation, parent. We never outgrow our need to censor what goes into our minds. The more good that goes in, the more good that comes out. Whatever kind of person you want your child, and yourself, also, to become is the kind you must display in your everyday life.

You can experiment with this by watching two very different movies together as a family. Watch the nasty, cruel, mean one in the evening before bedtime. Watch everyone as they do the evening chores and prepare for bed and then try to sleep. The next evening, watch one that has a good moral tone and/or good clean fun with happy ending, the happy cheerful sort of movie, and follow the same routine of chores and preparing for bed. The next morning, compare and think over the reactions and sleep of everyone. Just stop and think then what is the effect on the little children, on little boys and girls, two and three and four years old who are in the most important learning years of a person's life. If you don't learn the good stuff, then Satan has a foothold, and it will be very hard to get rid of.

Children react to a parent's true feelings at an early age. I never liked spinach. I never ate it, but because it is good for you, I felt I had to feed it to my children, so I faithfully bought spinach in the baby food jars and offered it to each one in turn. I know I tried to fool at least Mae and Terry, but they spit it right back at my fake smile. They sensed my true feelings!

Why is infidelity the cruelest possible way for a person to hurt his or her spouse? This one act is a sin against God, the guilty one's spouse, the guilty one's self, the guilty one's partner, and the unborn child the illicit union could produce, plus all the "innocent" bystanders, people who know what is going on but do nothing. This one act has long-lasting effects (e.g., the life of the innocent baby, even into the lives of that baby's babies)---- as God says "unto the third and fourth generation." Even if there is no child involved, it still stays with the people involved. God can and will, if asked, forgive, but the memory is not erased.

The chick hatchery was approximately 8 feet by 12 feet with 30 inch walls. The peak was probably 6 to 8 inches higher than eaves. The inside had a partition all across the middle. On the two long sides, partitions separated the area into individual areas with a nest next to the outer wall. The rest was for food and water. The nest areas were about 15 inches square. The roof was finished with solid roofing for the first two feet along the outside long walls. From there to the peak, doors made of framed chicken wire were placed to open for feeding and watering and closed to protect the hens from predators.

This hatchery could handle 20 hens and their egg settings. It could be made smaller by constructing only one side, or it could be two-sided but as short as you want or as a combination of the two.

In the spring when the old hens started getting broody (we always had roosters, so the eggs were fertile), we would pick fresh eggs and take a broody hen and 15 eggs to put under each hen. We put a hen in each one of those nests with a clutch of eggs. It would take 28 days for the eggs to hatch.

The wall between the nests and the feed and water areas was 4 inches high, so the hens could easily get to the feed and water. Each nest was covered by its own solid wood hinged door that protected the hens from the rain when in the nests. The feed and water area on each nesting side was covered with one door made of chicken wire to give the hens plenty of air and light. This was also the opening for filling the water and feed cans. The wall in the middle was approximately 24 to 30 inches high, and of course it was solid wood as were the dividers between the nests.

When they hatched, the chicks were moved to the chicken coop with a fenced-in area in front of it. We took the old hens and their babies and put them in that pen with feed and water. Later on, as I got older, we started ordering baby chicks from somewhere in Minnesota, I think. We'd ordered 100 babies. Of course, the family wasn't nearly as big then. We ordered both hens and roosters.

When they got old enough, we butchered the roosters and ate them as time went by. We kept this bunch of hens to lay eggs and the last year's hens were used for roasting or boiled chickens and other things. It was really nice, but a lot of work…. a lot of work!

We killed the past year's hens, as we needed them. We could tell if they were laying eggs or not by putting our fingers between the two bones on the back end. If it was wide enough for three fingers between those bones they were laying hens. If not, then the bones would be closer together, and we knew they weren't laying any eggs. They were just eating good food and went to the chopping block. They had to be cooked by boiling for chicken and noodles or chicken and dumplings or roasting in the oven, whatever-- they were not young and tender enough to be fryers.

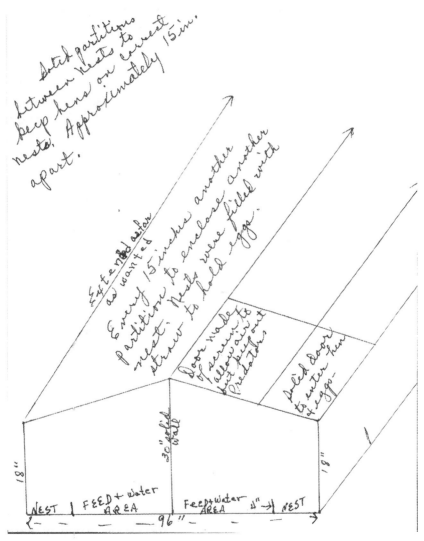

Add partitions between Nests to keep hens on correct nests. Approximately 15 in. apart.

Extended as far as wanted

Every 15 inches another partition to enclose another nest. Nests were filled with straw to hold eggs.

Door made of screen to allow air in but keeps out Predators.

Solid door to enter hen + eggs.

18"

30" solid wall

18"

NEST | FEED + Water AREA | Feed + Water AREA | 1" → | NEST

{ — — — — — — 96" — — — — }

Drawing of Hatchery.

Matthew 23:9 NIV tells us, "And do not call anyone on earth 'father' for you have one Father --- and He is in Heaven."

Of course, the ideal is two virgins, coming together in love and with God's blessing. The idea of a male virgin is ridiculed, but that is God's plan from day one. The first wedding couple were definitely both virgins. They were the perfect humans in the perfect environment, and they are our ideal even in this sinful, imperfect world in which we live. They are there for us to emulate. They came together in the presence of God, their creator. Because they had no sin, they were able to grow in knowledge and love of each other. They came to know the bliss of joining each other and God in creating another human. The male provided the sperm, the woman provided the ovum, and God provided the life (soul). Without God, the new creation would have been nothing but another animal. With God's presence and contribution, they were able to create another creation "in God's image."

We butchered beef and pork when the weather turned cold in the fall. We butchered hogs and steers that we had raised. The men killed the hogs, scalded them and scraped the skin to take all the hair off and leave a clean skin that made cracklings. A lot of lard came from them, too. Butchering is an art. The pig skins came through clean and completely hairless, so it could be a part of the food, too. The intestines were also cleaned completely so they could be used to make sausages. Dad always said he "Butchered for 40(or 41-or 42 or whatever), years and never cut a gut." It was a matter to be proud of, and we never heard of e-coli or had to worry about cooking the beef till it was like shoe leather.

The whole family would go to work cutting up the meat. We cut the fat in little chunks and put it on the stove in big kettles and rendered out the lard. It would have to get a little bit brown, and that was the sign that there was no moisture left in it. The cracklings were removed from the lard. We put the lard in big crocks and stored it in the root cellar to keep cool. That was our supply of shortening for the year.

We cured the ham and bacon using a big syringe to inject the "cure" which had been dissolved in water. I suppose the syringe held a pint of this fluid; we mixed up the cure and put it into the syringe barrel. We ran that long needle in parallel to the bones and squeezed the liquid into the meat as close to the bone as we could get and full length as the needle was withdrawn. We made sure to get the cure near the bones; otherwise, the hams and bacon spoiled before the cure worked its way all the way into the bone. After we completed that task, we mixed the brine in a wooden barrel. The hams and bacons were put into the brine and left for the length of time it took for them to be cured. They could then be taken out of the brine and hung up. I think it's odd that I don't remember where we stored the cured pork. I know it couldn't hang in the root cellar because that was too damp, and it would mold.

Cured meat would usually be too salty to eat without parboiling the meat before we cooked and ate it. To parboil it, we put the slices into a pan of cold water and brought the water up to where it would just barely begin to boil. Then, we removed the meat from the pan. The process would leech the salt out, and it would be good for using as we wanted, frying, boiling, or roasting.

Another thing we did was to cut the pork chops and fry them. We placed a layer of the melted lard into a big crock. It was melted so that it would let no air in--and then added a layer of the cooked pork chops, a layer of lard, a layer of pork chops, and then another layer of lard until we used up all of the pork chops. That way we could take them out and they still

tasted fresh. They would keep indefinitely, too. This was all stored in the root cellar that we had on every place we lived.

For the beef, we ate the heart and liver-with-onions on butchering day. We loved the heart the best! We liked the liver, too, but not a lot of it. But, of course we didn't waste it. It was eaten whether it was our favorite or not. Slices of heart ½" thick were dipped in flour with salt and pepper and slow fried until it was done through. Oh, so good! My favorite!

In the years since, I fairly regularly find myself hungry for liver and onions. It needs to be cooked right. Completely done but not hard and dried out.

In addition, we had the beef. We didn't save the tallow like we did on the pork as we had no use for it after we quit making our own soap. We butchered the beef and canned everything we couldn't use right away. Many times, we would wait until the middle of winter to butcher beef, so we could freeze it, and then we could just use it as we needed it. We sometimes stored hamburger the same as we stored the pork chops.

I hated like sin to can the beef. It would only keep a certain length of time without canning, and then we would have to do something else with it, so we canned an awful lot of the beef. Mostly, we just kept chickens around and butchered them as we could eat them for fresh meat.

We never went to church; I wish we had. I found out later that Mother read the Bible to all us kids before she died but it must have stayed with me because I have never doubted that God is in his Heaven and all is ok in His world. She gave me a solid foundation even though I don't remember it. Dad always told us we should choose our church when we grew up. None of us have ever chosen one certain church and remained loyal to it. Harry and I joined the Lutheran Brethren Church when we moved to Sidney, Montana. We were loyal to it but found we disagreed with some of their doctrine and finally left because of it. We had many good friends there and loved them and our pastor and his wife in spite of our disagreements. In traveling we began searching the local phone books for non-denominational Bible teaching churches and found they were much friendlier and warmer than the Strong Denominational churches—more loving and kinder in general.

Dad was a good singer, but by the time I got old enough to appreciate it, he had lost his voice and wasn't able to sing like he used to. I can kind of halfway remember him singing "Oh Danny Boy," or some of the old Irish songs. Then there was one, "The Baggage Coach Ahead," a sad, sad story about a man cradling his infant child who is crying for its deceased mother whose body is in "the baggage coach ahead". Anyway, Dad was getting pretty old by then. He had rheumatoid arthritis, I guess it was, and he was bedridden practically one whole winter. When he finally got through that, his hands were deformed. The cords of his fingers shrunk so that his little finger stayed folded. He couldn't open his hands. He had to get by with his hands like that.

With the stock market crash of 1929 and the horrible droughts of the Dirty Thirties, nothing dad did seem to pay the bills. It seemed like we were poor and just got poorer. Howard stayed home, but he wasn't much of a guy to go ahead and do things. Dad would not, absolutely, would not, take any welfare. I can remember during the Dirty Thirties how everyone, all the cousins, were getting the commodities, grapefruit and oranges and stuff from welfare, but boy, he just absolutely refused. He would not. There were times it was pretty, pretty skimpy, touch and go. That's the time we ate horse meat. Of course, it was perfectly all right. There is nothing wrong with eating horse meat. A lot of people in other countries do it all the time. It's stupid that you can't sell horses for horse meat here, too. These dumb idiots, animal worshipers, would rather see a horse slowly die by starvation.

Kids also had chores. We carried in the kindling or coal, as needed. We learned to chop wood, milk cows, churn butter, wash and dry dishes, help with cooking, canning, and butchering, and we washed clothes or did whatever needed to be done. We caught the chickens and killed, scalded and picked them, dug new potatoes or picked and shucked roasting ears. There were always things for kids to do. We carried wood (kindling) for the kitchen range. I don't remember where all the wood came from, but I do remember times when there was no more wood and Ora and I would take the old wash tub between us and walk out into the pasture to pick buffalo "chips." They made good hot fires, too, with little smoke unless you made a mistake and picked up a fresh still partly wet cow "chip."

The whole family worked to harvest the garden each fall. Potatoes, carrots, parsnips, turnips, rutabagas, onions, salsify (a root vegetable akin to parsnips) and any other root crop also went into the sand in the root cellar. There was a shelf in the root cellar. As I remember it, this one shelf was 4 feet wide by 8 feet long, and we placed the big crocks on the floor under the shelf.

We, children, were given jobs that would horrify modern day parents. I remember when I couldn't have been more than eight or nine years old, the year the gophers were so bad. They put holes in all the pastures and fields. The ones in the pastures endangered all the cattle and horses that ran though those pastures, and the holes in fields just made the ground so rough that it was dangerous for the machinery and the animals.

To counteract them, Dad bought strychnine-treated oats, and it was a job for Ora and I to each take a small bucket of it to the pastures and fields. We were to put three or four kernels of the treated grain down in the opening of every gopher hole. The gopher only had to eat one or two kernels to meet his demise. We had to make sure it was down deep enough that birds would not see it and eat it. We did it and lived through it with no ill effects. Gophers lived in towns, so we never had to cover the whole pasture or field. I remember it still seemed like a BIG area. The gopher problem never went away, but it did slack off.

Another problem was potato bugs. They liked to live on the potato vines and lay their eggs on the ground. When the worms hatched, they burrowed into the new potatoes and so left holes and bad spots there. To prevent this, we dissolved arsenic in water. Dad made brushes out of dried weeds tied together. We used these to dip into the arsenic and sprinkle the potato vines the bugs were eating, so they ate arsenic and died before they laid their eggs. With the potatoes growing underground the use of the arsenic was never a problem as it was never near the potato.

Lucille poisoning potato bugs

I don't know how it happened that Don and Harold Crites and I were left alone at Uncle Fred and Aunt Achsah's house. We decided to snare some gophers, so we got the twine and made a loop of it. We snuck up to a gopher hole where we had seen the gopher duck down inside. We were very quiet and carefully laid the noose around the opening and sat back at the far end of the twine and waited until the gopher came up to check. As soon as it popped its head up, we yanked the twine, and it tightened around the gopher's neck and killed him. I don't know who had the bright idea, but one of us suggested we butcher it. To be good butchers, we needed to cut his throat and let him bleed out. Every boy, worth his salt, had a jack knife in his pocket. Standard operating procedures, back then. We decided that we should do it right. We hung it up by the hind legs and skinned and gutted it. Well that looked like we had done a nice clean job and that it was ready to eat. We debated whether gopher meat was or was not edible. We finally decided that they were grass eaters like cattle, and cattle were edible, therefore, gophers would be. We took our "meat" into the house and proceeded to cook it and eat it. We never told any of the other kids about it! It tasted good, and no one got sick, so why take a chance on them telling the grown-ups? I suppose we were around nine to eleven years old then. Don't you just love cousins??

I must have been 7 or 8 when I walked with the rest of the kids to the reservoir on a hot summer day. We were still quite near the dam on our way home when I spied a water snake on the ground. I picked it up and carried it with me because I was interested in it and knew it was non-poisonous. I carried it in my hands until I saw an old bent up pail that still had a handle. I put my new pet in the bucket and carried it the rest of the way home where I excitedly showed it to Dad. He said, "Get that out of here and kill it."

The house sat on posts or rocks, so it was three or four feet off the ground making a nice shady place to get out of the heat of the day, so I took my snake and my tools under there. Well I don't exactly remember just how I killed it, but I decided I should butcher it. I used the knife I had to cut it open full length and watched with great interest and counted calmly as TWENTY-ONE babies crawled out of her and spread under the house. Then I made another big mistake! I told Dad about all those baby snakes. Once again, he was unimpressed and told me to "Kill every one of them!"

My memory of the incident ends there until in the middle of the night. Ora and I were in the girls' bedroom all alone as it was a Saturday, and all the older ones had gone to a dance. I started dreaming about the snakes. I dreamed I was in a buffalo wallow with all those snakes plus a lot more. They were all colors of the rainbow and were crawling all over me. I screamed and screamed until I woke Dad, and he came and quieted me and settled me back to sleep. That ended my friendship with snakes.

Cooking for those big groups was not easy. The one Sunday I took pictures happened entirely by chance. There were no phones to invite or warn. We just decided to go see Uncle John and Aunt Marian one Sunday morning, so we loaded into the truck. Ora, Floyd, and I rode in the back. Francis and Flossie with their families were already there. In a very short time, Fred and Achsah and several neighbors came. Aunt Marian took charge. She sent us kids to kill enough fryers for a meal, while the women started heating water, mixing a cake, and completing any other needed preparations for the meal. The kids scalded and picked the chickens so the women could singe them for pinfeathers and wash and cut them. We younger ones also had to go to the garden and dig potatoes. I don't remember if there were other vegetables to get from the garden. Very likely there was lettuce and radishes or onions. The men sat around visiting or drove around looking at crops until it was time to sit down and eat.

Back row: L to R: Evelyn Huestis, Lois Crites, Harold Crites, Leona Huestis, Roy Huestis, John Chvilicek, Jr, John Chvilicek, Frank Smith, Fred, Achsah Crites, Vern Crites, Alberta Crites holding Jean, Ken Shafer holding Verlyn, Lula Shafer, Carl Poore, Cleona Poore, Frank Huestis, ? Pester, Flossie Huestis. Second Row: Leonard Chvilicek, Jim Chvilicek, Dorothy Crites, June Crites, Gay Huestis, Rita Shafer, Alice Chvilicek, Lawrence Chvilicek, Dorene Crites, Norbert Chvilicek. Front Row: Marian Chvilicek, Vera Shafer, Bob Chvilicek, Keith Shafer, Dick Crites, Grandma Alice Huestis. (taken by LM Jensen)

Relatives at our house. The War (WWII) had started so no young men were here. Howard Smith, Frank Huestis, Jim Chvilicek, Vern, Don & Harold Crites. Group that gathered one Sunday at our house.

I was so used to being surrounded by cousins that I was very shy and tongue-tied around others when I went to school in town. At lunch time, country kids sat in their desks to eat their sack lunches and then played until school started again. Town kids went home to eat, then returned to rejoin the others. When I returned this one day, there were already half a dozen or so already there, and Elbert decided to tease me. I, of course, never answered which only encouraged him. He kept it up until I reached my limit, and I took him down in the middle of the room and sat on him. Guess I got his attention. He never teased me again, and I don't remember anyone else ever teasing me.

We became friends and graduated together with the class of 1941. I think we had around 20 in the third grade, but by graduation, there were only 10. The small towns had started fading away.

In good weather, we all met on the playground and played baseball. This included ALL grades from 1st graders up to and including the seniors who were actually men and women of 16, 17 or 18. Everybody played, and everybody helped the little ones. There was no such thing as a bully. They were under the eyes of the upper class-men. They never had a chance. I do wish schools were still like that. All ages associating with all other ages.

During my senior year, Floyd stayed with Lula and Ken to go to school in Gildford. Dad got me a job as helper at the Hingham Cafe and Hotel. I got my room in exchange for my work. I still fed myself. The New Deal out of Washington, DC started making jobs for high school seniors. I got the job of selling tickets at the basketball games. I also took care of the receipts and records and put them all away in the vault in the basement. It was a huge walk-in vault, and the door was unlocked in the morning and left open until closing time. I wonder if they still do that. For my work, I was paid $6 a month. I was thankful and frugal. Everyone wanted a pair of nylon stockings, and now I could buy myself a pair. Also thanks to that job, I was able to buy my class ring and also my senior pictures.

I went to one year of college on a scholarship. This was the fall that Pearl Harbor was bombed. Howard went into the Army and gave my address to a bunch of his buddies. They wrote to me. I answered all, but Harry was the only one I kept in touch with until the end of the war.

I spent one year as a teacher, and that was truly the worst mistake of my whole life. I had no idea how to teach and wasted that year of the children's lives. Thank God I never tried it again!

At conception, God breathes life (Spirit) into the mind-body provided by the human parents of this new creation. At birth, the three parts of this new creation are equal. The parents now have the monumental task of nurturing all three parts of this child. It is so easy to concentrate on the mind-body training. The body needs food and a warm place. To many, "correct food" can become a religion in itself. The Vegans are split into many sects---- The No Animals or Animal By-products including milk and eggs and butter, cream, or any foods using these products. There are many variations of diets. There are the No Carbs and its variations. The no-sugar, the no-fats, the no cooked foods, and the list goes on and on including the Liquid Balanced Meal diet. Each has its quirks. The body grows healthy and strong.

The mind is consciously nurtured. The body learns to speak clearly and perhaps to sing. Maybe to dance or defend oneself. Stories are read, and some parents teach their children to read at an early age. So the mind (will) is developed and nurtured.

What about the spirit? Here is the vital question. This is the time for the new spirit to grow, too. Have they heard that Jesus loves them? Have they learned that **everything** comes from God? That God created **everything**? That they can talk to Him at any time? That He answers prayer? That the Bible is the true word of God? That Jesus is the only begotten son of God? That Christmas is for celebrating the day God gave us the baby Jesus to save us from sin and is more about the giving than it is about getting? Also, that God's love covers us all. It seems to be so easy to always emphasize Gods rules and forget His Love.

When parents share all this and more about God, they are not giving Satan the chance to move into the child's mind and bend his will against God. As the child's spirit is nurtured, the day will come when he or she wants reassurance that God lives within. That is the time that the child asks about these things and decides it's time to be "born again." This is also a time of rejoicing for the parents. It shows them they have truly followed God's way. They have given the child a rock-solid foundation. It is not a guarantee that the child will never stray. He/she still has a will that needs nurturing and growth throughout life, but the parents have correctly done their duty in those early years.

Family and friend are simply defined. A family consists of a legally married wife and husband---- a man and woman with their blood-related children, plus other children legally adopted into the family. Friends are known outside the legal bloodlines and are loved dearly. They can be closer than a sibling. They can be a thousand miles away or next door, but they can be depended on to help at all times. They are willing to celebrate when you have received a special blessing or to cry with you when you are heartbroken. A friend freely forgives when hurt. A friend really likes you and thinks you are handsome, pretty, funny, kind, and all good things. The bad things are pretty well dismissed, or they help you change. Everyone hopes for all these traits in a family, but when they find them lacking, it is still mandatory to continue to love them, and forgive them and care for them as you are tied to them for life. To have a friend, one must **be** a friend.

Aunt Myra (Smith) Clemence told me that Dad had homesteaded in South Dakota, so he couldn't Homestead in Montana, but he owned his own horses and the machinery that was necessary for farming. The agreement was that Dad would do the farming for the rest of the group that came to Montana together, and with the pay they gave him, he would be able to buy land of his own. One thing after another went wrong, and he never got paid. So we always lived on rented land until someone bought it, and then we'd move to another farm a few miles away. I have a faint memory of Mother (she was already overweight) as she climbed to the top of all of the belongings piled into the hay wagon. I remember it was something that puzzled me as in the background was my very unhappy dad. I never asked for an explanation of these memories. Maybe because we were told not to talk about Mother after she died because it made Dad sad to talk about her.

I continue to be amazed whenever I remember the variety of dad's abilities. In my memory, there was never enough money to even be comfortable. But we were comfortable! Instead of hiring help we couldn't afford, he did a lot of skilled trade work himself. Some of the things he did and taught the boys to do it, too. He taught them animal tending skills like how to shoe horses, be an attentive stockman and doctor livestock. When it came time to process the livestock into food, dad taught the boys to make butcher knives and butcher ("I've butchered for 40 or 50 or 60 years and never cut a gut"). Other general ranch maintenance skills the boys learned from dad were blacksmithing (all kinds), woodworking and whittling, moving buildings, digging and building cellars and cisterns, rope making, carpenter, fencer, harvester, farmer. They even picked up some plumbing, catch rain-water and pump water into the kitchen. He firmly believed in going ahead and doing whatever needed to be done and doing it well.

When we moved from the place north of Hingham to the one north of Gildford, we had a granary. I suppose it was all wood, and it was probably 16 ft. x 24 ft., something like that. You didn't just hire someone to come in and load it up and move it. It was up to us. The granary was sitting on rocks for foundation. It was up off the ground, maybe a foot. We just took some big long poles and used them for levers and lifted it up so that we could get the running gears of a wagon under there and load it onto those wagon wheels and then hooked the tractor to it and moved it.

The devil can't touch the body as long as it is in the womb, but is waiting to start work as soon as the baby is born. Parents have a duty to start the counter-action immediately. Teaching about God and Jesus starts with the baby's birth. Some say it can start even before birth in the mother's womb---- singing, praying, or even talking to the baby. Some people call it dedication. Some call it baptism. Either way, the basic concept is of parents publicly promising to do all in their power to protect this soul from Satan until the child is old enough and his/her will is developed enough so the child is able to start developing that will to wholeheartedly follow God on his/her own. Parents are also asking God to help them raise their little one, and God never refuses.

Dad was laid up, Howard was in the Army, and the garden needed to be plowed. Me on the plow & Dorothy Crites on the horse.

We knew how to preserve food. We learned that early. We just were so used to canned food. We never had a refrigerator. We didn't have electricity or indoor plumbing.

We always had a big vegetable garden. Of course we had to can the peas, beans, and the corn for winter use. We had a good root cellar, so we could keep the carrots, rutabagas,---- all root crops ---oh, and we always had pumpkins and squash, too. We just kept trying to raise tomatoes, watermelon, and cantaloupe, but just had no luck with them. Dad liked to try new things. That's how we were introduced to salsify or "vegetable oysters." As I remember, salsify soup did taste like oyster soup. It was very good.

We canned in the old-fashioned way where we put it on the stove in a tub of water and kept the heat under it for hours, depending on what was canned---- corn, peas, beans or meat. I'm sure the meat took just as long or longer. The needed spices were added to the raw produce in the jars. Salt is all we added to the vegetables and salt and pepper to the meat.

We'd pick milk pails full of peas or beans then sit on the porch and shell the peas and snap the beans. After we got the gas-motored washing machine, we filled it about half full of real hot water. Then we'd dump a pail of peas in the hot water. After they wilted, we ran them through the wringer. The peas fell back into the water, and the pods went through to the garbage. We dipped the peas out, put them in jars, and canned them by the old hot water method.

We used the boiler (an oval shaped tub) for this as it would cover two holes in the stove-top. It took, I think, two-and-a-half to three hours in this boiling water for each load. We kept this fire going for the full time because it was necessary in order to be sure the jars would be sterile. It was also the hottest time of the year. No fans. No refrigeration. No air conditioning. Canning was very hot work!

The dill pickles were made in a big 10-gallon crock. We washed the cucumbers and put them in the crock. Then we added a layer of dill and poured the vinegar, water and salt mixture over it all. Next we added a fitted and weighted board to hold them down. With the board that fit down inside, and weighed down with a clean rock that we put there, cucumbers were held down in the juice. As we picked more cucumbers, we washed them and added them to the crock with more dill each time and added more brine as it was needed. They cured in there, and they kept indefinitely. Later, as the family got smaller, once they cured, we transferred them to jars.

We did the fruit and tomatoes in open kettles. Jams and jellies were usually easier, too. Except choke cherries. We all loved chokecherry syrup, but we also wanted jams and jellies. It was never a problem making syrup. We put the cooked chokecherries through a sieve or a press or whatever it was called to remove the seeds. Next, we measured juice and sugar in the right proportions and put it on the stove to boil for 15 minutes to sterilize it and melt the sugar. Next was pouring it into the sterile jars and sealing. Very simple, right? Cool them overnight and check each jar to be sure it was sealed, and jars of fresh syrup took a trip to the root cellar.

That was the syrup, BUT jelly was an entirely different story. The recipe was as simple as the one for syrup, but the proportions were different. We used less water in cooking the chokecherries and more sugar in making the jelly. The idea was boil the mixture until it would "jell." This could go on and on. When we decided it was ready, we sealed it like the syrup and hoped it would really be jelled when we wanted to use it. Most times it didn't. It wasn't until years later that I saw Barb (Terry's wife) using pectin from the store that I realized what we had needed. Back then there was no money for unnecessary items, anyway.

Of course, we boiled the lids and the jars for 15 minutes so that they were sterilized. We were very, very careful not to leave anything on the rim of the jar because the least bit of dirt or grease gave the germs a foothold and eventually the food spoiled. As long as I can remember, we used the two-piece lids consisting of a flat piece that had a ring of sealant around the underside. This flat piece was then held in place by a ring that screwed onto the top of the jar. We handled the lids with tongs, so we didn't get any germs from our hands onto the lids. That was the flat part that went on the top of the jar. We just never had food spoil. We always did a good enough job that it did not spoil.

I remember when we were north of Hingham or maybe it was Rudyard. Dad put up ice in the ice-house, so we could have ice all summer. He must have raised flax because it seemed flax straw was used to pack the ice. I don't know why it was always flax straw, but that's what they packed around the ice to keep it, so it wouldn't melt over summer.

We had a big, 5-gallon ice cream freezer, hand-cranked of course. The house we lived in then had a very nice big porch. About the only memory I have about that place was the big family get-together on July 4th. Dad always said we should have new potatoes and peas and fresh fryers for the 4th. This time we also had home-made ice cream made in the big 5-gallon freezer sitting on the big old porch with everyone who was willing taking turns cranking. The kids cranked at first, but as the ice cream got thicker, it required the men with their added strength.

Another cause for celebration was when the roasting ears matured. We'd fill the boiler (the oval shaped tub) with water and bring it to a boil. By that time, the ears of sweet corn would be ready. They were put in the boiling water, and as soon as the water boiled again, we had dinner, (noon).

The cow pasture north of Gildford was in the Milk River breaks. One of the cows ate her way up a short canyon near the river, and by the time she got to the end of it, the sides had closed in on her. The space was so narrow, she couldn't turn, and she didn't know enough to back out, so she was stuck there. Magpies found her before Howard did. They ate holes in her back where the grubs had settled. Howard had to rope her and drag her out backwards. She survived with axle grease put in the holes to protect her from flies and magpies.

A curse is something to be avoided. *Of course*! Still male humans have expected women to live up to the curse of Genesis 3:16. "To the woman he said, 'I will greatly increase your pains in childbearing. In pain you shall bring forth children, yet your desire shall be for your husband and he shall rule over you'". That's a general quote but I like the way The Message says it "---but he'll lord it over you." The Message. First of all, we need to recognize that sin is the cause of this curse because of the first disobedience in Eden. Adam and Eve had everything a person could possibly want: a home, a work, family, and love, but Satan was already alive and well then as he is today. Satan appeared as the most beautiful of all beings and with his slick tongue convinced Adam and Eve to disobey God's one rule. God changed that beautiful thing into a slimy slithering snake that had no feet or hands, so he had to crawl on his belly. God had to remove Mankind from the garden before he also ate from the Tree of Life and so lived forever.

Because of this original sin, the consequence is pain in childbearing, sometimes in one form sometimes in another, and maybe in copulation or morning sickness or actual birthing. At all times, it is a man's duty to love and treat his wife with love in each instance as much as humanly possible. At the same time, there is this desire for her husband. This is not quite simply a desire for sexual contact as so often interpreted. There is the yearning for physical contact, yes, and it should be expressed most often as hugging, being held tenderly, a gentle kiss, kindness, even a pat on the shoulder, a smile across the room, peace of mind, (do we have food and shelter? Will we be able to care for this precious baby? Will her husband love and care for her and the baby while she is unable to?). This desire for her husband is not for more and more sexual contact, as rapists are known to have told the victim, "You know you want it." To be raped is the most heinous thing that can ever happen to a woman, the greatest insult a man can inflict on his wife is to go to a woman other than his wife for sex. The same goes for the wife who goes to a man other than her husband.

People say it's not fair that God provides only one way to get to Him. Before that one way opened, there was **no** way. *Without the one way, there is still no way.* The one and only way to get to God is through His son, Jesus, who is our savior. Praise God that He has given us a way. It isn't like going to a crowded restaurant where you have to wait for your turn to get in and be waited on. In this place of business, service is instantaneous no matter where you are or how many are wanting the same thing!

God gave the law to his chosen people, so they could know what was right and good from what was wrong and hurtful. They were to follow this because the results are always beneficial to those who faithfully live right. The law also warns of the harm that *always* results from doing the wrong.

Picture the Triune God watching as one of his creation stood at the edge of a cliff. It is one of God's laws that if you jump off that cliff, you are going to be hurt or killed depending on how high the cliff is, et cetera. People say that's not God, that's gravity, it's not in the Bible. Of course not. It is learned so early in life and so easily that God had no need to write it out. Besides, what is gravity and who made it?

1. Don't stop breathing
2. Don't jump off a cliff
3. Don't cut yourself
4. Don't touch a red-hot item
5. Don't stay under water too long
6. Don't let heavy things drop on you
7. Don't get too much sun
8. Don't stop breathing

There are myriad unwritten "Thou shalt nots." These are things that are harmful if not handled correctly. Why didn't God add them to the list in the Bible? Common Sense. Everyone learned early in life that the consequences were sudden, uncomfortable, and unavoidable. Then there are the others with equal or even more serious consequences, but those consequences were not so evident. Some are delayed for years and damaging to more than one person. Consequences can be mental, physical, or spiritual. Any one or a combination of any two or three. Because they are less obvious, God wrote them out to aid his created. Rather than appreciate his kindness and care, humanity has said, "I don't believe it, and I can do it because I want to and I feel like it's OK. There really isn't anything wrong with it if you feel good doing it." Now they are wondering why everything is getting so messy!!!

The result of sin is death. Here we have one of God's written laws. The results are as sure as harm from jumping from a cliff, but they are not so obvious. We have to realize that if God said it, it is fact, and act accordingly. That is why Jesus came as the ultimate teacher. He has taught that repentance can raise the sinner from Death. It doesn't protect the sinner from having to live with the results of sin, but God the helper will give this sinner Grace to manage it and eternal life to enjoy forever.

I am sad and frightened and quite frankly horrified at the ignorance of our people in this generation. When I was young, we were taught right and wrong. We had rules and regulations to guide us. Any time there was doubt as to what was right, there was a Book to read that would explain it for us. Sin was called sin not "another life-style." We had the 10 commandments of God, and no matter how much we refused to admit we were doing wrong, we still realized there was a right and wrong where the right was good, and wrong was evil! We knew deep down that God was in Heaven, and He was always there for us.

It must be so frightening to grow up today not knowing right and wrong, to be surrounded by adults who are unwilling to fight evil and encourage right, because they don't think there is real evil and a real Rock to save us, God. There is One that we can always depend on who is real and who never leaves us!

Some blame God for causing all the sickness, hatred, floods, fires, and wars. That is completely wrong. Humanity is definitely to blame. God did not make us robots to automatically worship Him without feeling or knowing. Instead, He made these marvelous bodies to walk upright with Him, to visit with Him, to worship Him, and love Him in return. After making this marvelous, miraculous body with only two feet but also hands, He breathed Soul into us. This is the only way we differ from animals. We were told we should, with His help, create more humans, care for the animals and plants but never to worship them. He promised to be with us; He would never leave us nor forsake us; He would walk with us in the Garden of Eden.

God does not go back on his word, so he is still with us every second of every day wherever we may be. Those who are denying God's very existence still have God at their side. He is still guiding, He still loves, and He is still reaching out to all. It strikes me as a sign of God's sense of humor. Here is this puny impotent little human rattling on and on about there is no God. I'm doing this myself. I don't need any help from an imaginary God. I can live my life, and all the while, God is right there watching with a fond look like a parent watching a child take his or her first wobbly step.

The body parts are interdependent. Maybe you had a broken arm and immediately that hand is also inactive. The other hand is forced to take on extra work. Even with the extra work, there are still things that are impossible for the healthy hand to do. Certainly, it can't wash its own elbow. The left hand of a right-handed person finds it nearly impossible to write. One hand alone even has trouble with such a necessary act as feeding the body. Then if the left hand gets angry and refuses to do more than "my share," the whole body is really in trouble.

Churches too often become the pastor's private dictatorships. He/she decides everything about the church. Forgetting the job is to Shepherd, to be a leader not a pusher or tyrant. It is too easy to get an inflated idea of the importance of oneself and opinions. Humans in power are prone to want more, more, more.

Harry's Dad, Soren, gave Harry 10 head of young cows, so he could get a start. We lived there with Soren at his homestead when Harry was first discharged from the Army. Betty and Earl were there, too, until they fixed up the house over on the Gaine's place and moved over there. We stayed with Soren till Soren's brother, Jens, died, then we moved to his place. Barney and Jeanette came back from Alaska, and they lived together with Soren on the "home place" until he passed away. We bought the Hans Blazek Place and a railroad section. We had three sections of land there. We finally got electricity in 1952 and inside plumbing a couple years later. I had all four kids potty trained before we had indoor plumbing so I was through washing diapers. That was before the day of disposables, too.

We built the big dam on Section 35, and it held over 400 acre feet of water. We had the water rights on that creek. Harry, Earl and Barney put all their land together and formed a Sub Chapter "S" family corporation called 3J Herefords for short. 3J put a pump in at the dam and pumped water to ditch-irrigate the field. The field was a flat between the two creeks there. About a hundred and thirty-acres in the field was fit for irrigation. This was fine as long as we got enough spring run-off and summer rains to keep the dam full, but we went into a dry spell, so with no water to irrigate with and of course no grass for native hay, we went looking for a hay base. That's when we found the land down by Sidney, and 3J bought it. Harry was the one who liked the irrigating, so we moved to Sidney.

Recent Family Reunion Lions Camp Marian, Montana 2000

God loves us. Everyone has heard this so often, the wonder of it gets away, gets lost in the busyness of everyday life. God is with us every minute of our lives, no matter what we are doing---no matter where we are---no matter our mood. Have you ever stopped to really think about these aspects of God? He is there at conception to breathe Life-Soul-Spirit into us. Otherwise we'd be animals. He has shared your creation with your parents at the instant you were conceived. God stayed with you throughout your time in your mother's womb. Aren't you glad they didn't decide on abortion? God was beside you as you were born. He helped you through the precarious passage as you moved out into the fresh air and the loving arms of your parents. God was with you as you grew and developed while you were at home with your parents. He loved you and stood beside you when you left home. He stayed with you as you grew and moved on in life. He watched you all the times you made all those mistakes, while you grew and often forgot or ignored Him. That time you were in a strange area? You wanted to do something that you knew was not right and excused yourself with, "No one will ever know," but He was there all along, watching. He loved you and stayed beside you whether you loved him in return or ignored him. He was still beside you and never once stopped loving you. He knows you inside out, front to back, day and night, happy or miserable; He has stayed beside you! And He is here NOW!

I know one time the corporation was $500 short, and I could not find where that $500 went. I went through all the statements for the whole year. I never could find that, so I finally went in to the bank. I told the president, "There is this discrepancy between my balance and your balance, and there is $500 missing from our account." He told me they had a lady called "Jeraldine" who was a whiz at getting to the bottom of this kind of problem. "We will call her, and if you take it to her, she will figure it out for you." So "Jeraldine" looked through my records and went to work on it. After she worked on it for a while, she suggested that if I wanted to finish my other business in Glendive, to just go ahead, and she would find the problem while I was gone.

When I returned a couple hours later, she reported, "I just can't figure it out either. I don't know what happened." I just gave up. We lost the $500. It wasn't but two or three months later that the bank discovered they were short of funds. The law says bank workers MUST take a two-week vacation, in consecutive days, once a year. But "Jeraldine" would let a friend use one or two of her vacation days and of course, get the days back during a long weekend or something of the sort. In that two weeks, any fancy bookkeeping in a person's work would show up. By never taking a full two weeks at a time, good ol' Jeraldine was able to abscond with a goodly sum before she was caught. So guess where our $500 went? I can guess. We never got it!

I was a conscientious bookkeeper to the point of (looking back) ridiculous. One month when making out the paychecks, which at that time, included figuring the withholding tax, the total for each check amounted to so many dollars and 99 cents, so I wrote the three checks and turned them over to each one of the guys. When I got the bank statement, they were $0.03 short. I tell you, I worked for days trying to find those $0.03. When I finally found them, it was the bank's fault! The checks I had made out for the men were so many dollars and ninety-nine cents, and the teller who had entered it had rounded off the blamed thing to the nearest dollar.

One of the first things I learned when I became a Christian was that we should tithe 10% of our money. Of course, we were so broke 90% of the time that 10% might have been only a few dollars, but it seemed like a lot to us. We soon found out that when we gave the Lord his 10% as we were supposed to, that we had no business spending in the first place, he stretched the other 90% to cover everything we needed.

There were times when I was completely flabbergasted with our private account once we started tithing. We would have more money in our account than my figures said we had. I knew the extra funds did not come from the bank. Banks don't do that. Your account may be short, but the bank never puts additional money in your account. I don't know how many times I thought I was broke, and I would get our statement from the bank, and there was still money in our account. I don't know where it came from to this day. It happened at least 4 or 5 times when I was just really at the very end of my rope and didn't know how I was going to get by. I would check out how much was in the bank, and there would be $100 or even more depending on how much I needed, and it was always enough. God always came through.

I came to the Lord when I was 48 years old, but it was several years later before Harry finally completely turned his life over to the Lord and began to live his life for Him. He had done way too much drinking throughout his life, and it was such a blessing for me when he finally quit. Once he stopped drinking, he wasn't interested in even a glass of wine or mug of beer. He was done with it! I still don't live as I think I should, but praise God, I have Jesus as my savior. I'm far from perfect but praise God, I'm not the same as I was ten, twenty or thirty years ago or even as I was yesterday. Harry and I will meet again. I pray that our children and grandchildren all come to know the peace and joy that comes from knowing what we've got. When you've got the Lord and know that He's there for you at all times, when you turn your life over to him, everything that happens then acts for your good. You may not think so at the time, but if you just truly, truly live for Him and then have bad things happen, you know that there is a reason behind it. It isn't some random thing. Although sometimes things happen to us that we can never understand until we're in Heaven and face-to-face with the Lord. We are safe in His care, and He will carry us through. He is there. He is dependable. Praise God! He takes care of us. The longer we love Him, the sweeter life becomes!

When my brother, Howard, first entered the army, he was sent to Texas for training, and that's where he and Harry met. Harry was from Circle in eastern Montana, and Howard was from Gildford, which was in the north central part of Montana.

Of course, in those days, everybody was supposed to write to the soldiers. I think there were five of them that wrote to me, and I answered all of them, but Harry was the only one I wrote to throughout the war. When the war was over, he came looking for me.

As soon as the war was over, those of us who had worked in the shipyards quit our jobs and headed for home. I rode with Alice and Lavern. They had a trailer to haul their belongings and made room for me in the car and my boxes in the trailer, and we left for Montana! They stopped in Kalispell where they spent the rest of their lives. I went to Polson and visited Lula and family for a while then to Sunburst to visit my friend Junie who lived there with her husband John Richter and two boys.

Once I got to Montana again, I had to find a job. Sunburst was just five or six miles south of the Canadian border. They needed help at the café in the Sunburst Hotel, so I started work there. Harry finally located me at Sunburst. He had stopped at Lula and Ken's. That was the last address he had.

A bunch of us had gone to Cutbank (a bigger town with nicer places) for dinner, and so I wasn't there when he got there that evening by bus. He took a room at the hotel. The next morning, I went to work at the restaurant. They told me that somebody was looking for me. I went to his second-floor room and knocked on his door. When he opened the door, we just looked at each other and opened our arms, and we both knew this was IT!

On the 25th of December, 1945, we were married in Glendive where Harry's mother lived at the time. We visited out at the ranch with Soren, and Betty and Earl then went to Glendive to visit Isabel at her house. We went ahead and planned our wedding there. The pastor at the Lutheran Church there had been the pastor at Hingham when I was going to high school. I was president of the Luther League then.

It was quite a coincidence to find him in Glendive when I planned my wedding. In recent years, they built a new big church in Glendive and sold the old building. It was a brick building which has been turned into a private home. The people who bought it have used it to raise quite a large family, some of them adopted.

Wedding picture of Harry & Lucille (Smith) Jensen
– December 25, 1945

Harry didn't have his discharge from the Army yet. He was on leave for a month. After the wedding, we visited around Montana until it was time for Harry to report to the Army at Camp Crowder. The soldiers were given points according to their Army position and length of stay to determine who received a discharge or were kept in for longer. Harry was told at first that he didn't have enough points and so he had to stay on, but then after we had been in Camp Crowder for 2 or 3 weeks, the Army changed its point system and Harry was one of those who had enough points for a discharge. Harry and I, along with Bernard and Ceola Trinity, were given the men's own discharge papers to travel to Fort Leavenworth in Kansas where Harry and Bernard were discharged. There must have been twenty others, but they had a sergeant with them who handled all their paperwork. We got up to Fort Leavenworth and were there for 2 or 3 days when the guys got their discharge papers, and everybody headed for home. Bernard and Ceola went to Michigan, but we kept in touch through the years. Bernard passed away around 2001 and now Harry has gone, too. The last I heard, Ceola was still living, but she had moved to a different place. We never did get to visit again, but we always talked about it. Harry and I went to Billings and then over to Big Timber where Harry had worked before he went into the army.

The Faw family members were all good friends. He had worked for a Faw girl and her husband before he left Big Timber. The three Faw brothers were good buddies of Harry, and they really had a lot of fun together before they went into the service. All three came out alive and were not really crippled up. They were very, very blessed!

Love covers so many actions and feelings. Respect for the loved one's sexuality - feminine traits in a woman and masculine traits in a man. Women don't need to be physically strong because God made men to be naturally physically strong. A man is to recognize his strength as a mandate from God for protecting the mother of his child both before and after its birth. Too often, men believe the lack of physical strength makes one mentally weak when the opposite is true. A wise man talks to his wife. He asks for her opinion, and she can ponder a problem while nursing a baby and during other quiet times during the day. Such times can be scarce if several children are born close together, but couples must find time to talk. In a blink of an eye, the little ones leave home and couples need to feel comfortable with each other at this time, It should be the happiest time of their lives.

No one ever told me anything about being born again. Lula gave me a King James Bible when I graduated from the 8th grade. I was a person who read every book, and I mean every book, I got my hands on. I read magazines, newspapers and encyclopedias. I started to read the Bible several times for different reasons. First, I thought I should. Second, I had nothing else to read, and finally, I wanted to be a Christian.

When we started spending the school years in Hingham, I went to church when we couldn't get home for the weekend. I went to Luther League Youth Group. I became the president. I still didn't feel sure and safe, and I still didn't read the Bible.

I graduated second in my class and went to Havre my first year of college. It was a big disappointment as all of the studies were a rehash of what I'd had in grade school and high school. I can remember one thing I learned, how to pronounce words according to the accent marks in the dictionary. Two things I wanted to do from childhood was paint pictures and write books. My 8th grade teacher convinced me that I would never be able to paint and my literature teacher convinced me I could never write so I settled for being a teacher. I was worse than no good at that. I learned from that experience that a poor teacher is always over paid.

Ora was working in Seattle for Boeing as a riveter building aircraft, and Alice and Lavern with their 3 kids lived in Vancouver, Washington and worked at Kaiser shipyards. The shipyard was hiring, so that's where I went and applied. I've already told how they needed welders and they paid me while I trained. We worked seven days a week. We made those carriers as fast as they could be made, and we did a good job of it. The only men were supervisors and crew bosses with a few "4-F" older married men. We women didn't mind. We knew we were doing good necessary work and getting paid a living wage.

Lucille in leathers that were worn for welding
Kaiser Ship Yard, Vancouver, Washington

Lucille's shipyard Identification

God made man. True. God made male humans first. False. The word "man" has changed in meaning over the years, when it was written, it meant human. It meant a sexless human or person. That human being was made with a will and being human, was unsatisfied with the status quo. Imagine that here is this person in the very presence of God himself and a garden that provided every physical need for the taking and still "I want. I need. I wish". God being the loving caring God he is said "Okay," and put the man to sleep. There in front of him were all the parts needed to make another person. God divided the shell into two separate shells and proceeded to take parts from the one to put into the other. God decided how much of each talent was going to each shell and with each talent he also inserted a sense of responsibility to use these talents or abilities. God didn't necessarily evenly divide every one of these talents, and one talent was no more important than another. God divided these according to need for the work God planned you to handle. Each might be able to carry out God's plan for his or her future. A man and a woman will become separate, but each is unfinished, and it is this yearning to be complete that brings a man and woman together in marriage. Sex alone cannot ever do it. There are too many facets to each man and woman.

There are no male or female jobs in marriage except in parenting. The man supplies the sperm then loves and protects a mother and baby. The woman supplies the ova and the growing space for the baby during the next 9 months and anything else she is able. Work at this time needs to be shared as much as possible without the old division your job, my job. If all jobs are shared, mutual respect for both jobs, grows, and each handles as much as he/she is capable. It's too easy for one or the other to make a show while doing a slipshod job, so they can show how easy it is or make the other parents so disgusted, "I'd rather do it myself." Wrong, wrong, wrong.

The first contract with God comes to each person who accepts Christ as Savior. This should be the time one realizes how close God is at all times - the full meaning of omnipresent, omniscient and omnipotent. Only God can be any one of these things, and He is all three at all times, too. To realize this, to really know it, transforms a person. To know you have a bit of this in yourself, that He is in you and around you all the time. You may be miles from all people, completely at a loss as to which way to turn, worried and afraid of what will happen next. He will take care of you! He will talk to you. He will take your hand and show you the way, guide you into the correct way. A pretty good Guy to enter a contract with!

A couple getting married is entering a different Covenant, and I think what applies to one applies to the other. God now treats them as a single unit, and He is all three of these "omnies" in the middle of a true loving marriage. He is there at each conception. He is with both and is the glue that keeps them and binds them into one. As each person goes about his or her daily routine, that bond keeps him or her together and blends two into one. Humans being what they are, it doesn't happen overnight for most couples. And Satan is always near also, just waiting for his chance. This makes daily devotions and open conversations truly necessary!

Grandpa Harry's cold-induced asthma developed into emphysema. He had started smoking when he was 14 and never quit until he was in his 70s. Besides that, being a farmer in dryland country, he drove a Cat D8 in front of a plow to break up native sod. At harvest time, there, was always a granary that needed cleaning or some other dirty dusty job. He used to come in from a day in the field so covered with dirt that all that showed were his eyes and his teeth if he grinned. I tried to talk him into using a mask, but he never would. It finally caught up with him, and he gradually could fight it no longer and passed away at home on May 6, 2010.

I never knew a person could hurt so bad.

I spent that winter in Texas with Deb and Don but knew I'd never be able to take care of the house and yard in Sidney. I sold it and bought a travel trailer, which I moved to Richey. Sidney was in the middle of the oil boom, and parking spaces there weren't to be found for love or money. I settled in Richey and thought I was set for life. My lot was on the very edge of that nice little town, so it was almost as good as living in the country. The plan was to spend the winters in Texas and the rest of the year in Montana. I was 88 years old, but I was a healthy 88. I decided to take my van and embark on a road trip around Montana to visit the relatives I had left and see the country. My route took me from Richey to Sidney, to north of Brockton where I visited the Don Dahlberg family. Don's first wife was cousin, Gaye Huestis. I really loved it. I enjoyed the driving, and seeing family again is my favorite form of recreation. The route then stopped in Poplar, at the Percolater owned by the Dahlberg girls. Both have other names now, but that is the easiest way to identify them. I really got filled up with my favorite drink—Coffee!

In Chinook, I stayed a couple days with cousin LaRena Crites Stewart. I got to visit with her son, too. When I arrived in Havre, I took advantage of the hospitality offered by cousin Darlene Olson. She is the daughter of cousin Lois Crites Olsen. Again I got to visit her sisters.

My next stretch went along the Hi-line (High-way 2) through all those little towns. They have gotten so much smaller. All along there, they have had to consolidate like Hingham and Rudyard. Just six miles apart, they've had to go to a grade school in Hingham and a high school in Rudyard. So the old Hingham Rangers that Alice, Lula and Velma were part of when they won the Championship are no longer. There just aren't enough people in the area.

The homesteaders thought they were rich and going to make it big with their 320 acres but soon found out that in prairie country, one cow alone required about 30 acres, and that was normal rainfall not accounting for the years of drought or hail or both. A lot of those 320 acres had no natural year-round water. The lucky ones had a spring that flowed year-round, but it wasn't a sure thing. Mother Nature thinned the homesteaders out fast. At Gildford I turned north and drove past "the old Crites Place" where uncle Fred and Aunt Achsah had lived, and we had many clan get-togethers.

The empty house was near collapse.

Out past where we once lived, nothing. Where we built the house was a solid field of golden wheat waving in the wind. No buildings, no dam, nothing. The old Fairchild schoolhouse was also gone. I did see it later, but it was still empty and sitting in a deserted farmyard.

It was wonderful to arrive at the VandeSandts and visit Bud and Margaret and Hap and Sonya. This was a neat farmstead with two neat well-kept homes. The VandeSandts aren't really relatives unless you go waaaaaay down on the shirttail, but they are part of the few who still live there. Bud and my younger brother, Floyd, were best friends, and Floyd requested his ashes be scattered along the trail down the cutbanks into the Milk River bottoms. This is on a part of the VandeSandt land, so we consulted with Bud to get it done. We had a memorial service there with Bud doing the speaking. Then Floyd's son, Doug, scattered the ashes, and Floyd's daughters and grandchildren laid roses at the head of the trail.

The boulders at the trailhead were so much the color of the surroundings that Bud decided something different needed to be found, and he did it. The boulder he found was gold sandstone about 3 ½ feet long and maybe 15 inches in diameter. Bud moved it a few miles from its native location to the trail head and placed Floyd's plaque on it.

Floyd Smith memorial plaque
overlooking the Milk River.
Photo by G. VandeSandt

Floyd Smith on Paint

I was traveling by GPS all this time, so when I was ready to leave the VandeSandts, I checked with my GPS and found out I was in Canada!!!! I knew I wasn't, but there was no convincing my GPS! It corrected itself once I was back on the hi-line!

My next visit was Hazel Idland. She lived in Fairview and was very ill. You couldn't tell by talking to her; she was still her old cheerful, loving and kind self. From there, I drove to Ulm (by the way, all these places are still in Montana). Two of cousin Roy Huestis' daughters live there. Each one has her own small ranch where she raises horses and dogs. Peggy was an RN who joined YWAM when she was younger, then she and Bonnie opened the Goldstone, a home for the Assisted Living in Great Falls. I'm proud of all my family. Every one of them that I've known have been hard working and honest. The women are also hard workers and if need to, have done well on their own. We may not be nationally known, but people, who know us, recognize that.

After visiting Peggy and Bonnie, I decided I really wanted to go back to see Hazel one more time, and I'm so glad I did. She was fading fast, but I got to say "Goodbye" before it was too late. I went on my way to Kalispell to visit my sister Alice's daughter. In two or three days, I got word Hazel was gone. Jeanne and I had a good visit. She has also grown closer to the Lord, and He has healed so much of her diabetes. She is still training horses and her granddaughters in barrel racing! After a few days, I moved on to another niece, Floyd's daughter and family at Lewistown. Tracie and Jim's daughter, Kar, still live and work in Lewistown, but the other two, Cary and Lacie, are married with families of their own and live and work in Billings. With Jim and Tracie, I got to spend a couple days at the local county fair.

That is one of the best parts of country living, going to fairs. Of course, I was pretty well filled up with all of it when we were showing Herefords, and our kids were showing in 4-H. We used to go to several different county fairs with the show cattle. We did that until Jensen Brothers split up into three family corporations after Barney's death. We became KN Inc. with Soren's original brand and stayed with commercial Herefords. It wasn't very long before Harry's health made it impossible for us to keep it up, so we put the irrigated land at Sidney up for sale - except for 48 acres we kept as a hay base for the dry land at Circle.

Back to my tale in Lewistown. I had planned and wanted to go to Helena and then follow the interstate with stops along the way back to Glendive and Sidney, but my age caught up with me. I decided I didn't have enough oomph to go on, so I made a beeline for home to rest up for my trip to Indiana for the Smith Family Reunion in Indiana.

These Smiths were all descendants of my dad's oldest brother, James. We always called him Uncle Jim, and he lived in Arkansas, but several of his children had stayed behind in Indiana when he moved to AR. I landed at the airport in South Bend, Indiana and was met by three cousins I had never seen before. They were granddaughters of my uncle Jim. I think the nicest thing about families is how easy it is to visit with complete strangers. They had grown up knowing each other and their families while I had never heard of them except by mail. And not much of that, but when we met, it was like 'old home week'. I really had a ball.

We did some genealogy searches because that was the area where our closest common ancestor had bought some land from an Indian, and we were able to take pictures of the contract that was recorded at the courthouse. Our James Finley Smith and his wife, India Jane Darby Smith, had settled there before roads or anything. He had, through the years, owned a gristmill, a lumber mill and an inn. He also was on some county boards. He built the first house of sawn lumber in that area according to the historical info we found. We also found the land where my Dad's maternal grandparents, Andrew and Nancy McClellan Shaw, had lived. "In 1829 they moved to Wills Township where he purchased from the Indians part of section six, and this is where they made their home for the remainder of their lives." This is quoted from Glenn E Robinson's *Records of Andrew and Nancy Shaw*. This is one ancient record I was able to photograph.

I've been thinking of some of the old sayings that were used all the time when I was a kid. Many of them were gross, and I'm not sure I want to pass them on but will pass these along:

She /he is snooty.

Never let a baby see itself in a mirror before it is a year old.

Break a mirror is seven years of bad luck.

She/he thinks her/his s—t doesn't stink, but her/his f____ts give her/ him away.

A black cat crossing your track is bad luck.

Stand tall and proud as a young pine.

Skinny as a rail.

Fat as a pig.

Never walk under a ladder.

She's got one in the chute.

She's about to calve.

Tiny preemie----almost a crop failure.

No more after twins----when I started catching two at a time, I just coiled my rope and laid it on the shelf.

Sure shot---father of many children, close together.

Fertile myrtle----mother of many children close together.

Tune the old cow died on----bad music.

Dirty thirties---dust storm years.

Shackin'---living together but unmarried.

"Every little bit counts," the old man said as he peed in the ocean.

As alike as two peas in a pod.

"Never cut towards yourself," the old maid said. The rest, "I did once, and look at the slit I got," was usually just inferred.

I'm sicker than a horse.

Got a belly like a skimmed-milk calf or a beer-belly.

Worth his/her salt= a pretty good kid.

I had a terrible brain infection or something in September, 2012. The doctors never did agree on what exactly happened. There have been three theories developed since. One was that the brain infection was caused by long use of tap water for sinus rinse. I had been doing that for years, faithfully, every morning. Only by my own reading did I find out that was a possibility.

Another problem was low potassium. They loaded me with potassium, and in a few days, that was back to normal. Fine. But I wasn't back to normal. I got better slowly but very slowly.

The kids decided I couldn't live alone any more, and the three in Montana didn't have room for me to have private quarters in their homes, so Deb and Don invited me to Texas to live in their home. They made a little apartment in their house, so I could have privacy and some independence, and I became a Texan; not easy for a 'dyed in the wool' Montanan of some eighty-eight years! I did fairly well for a while with ups and downs. My Texas Dr. discovered I was also low on salt. I had been on a low-salt diet since I was about 40-45 years old for fluid retention along with diuretics. My Texas Dr. had my blood tests done and called me up and told me to go to the emergency room, and tell them she sent me, and I was low on salt. They put me right in the hospital, and the Dr. on call told me I was on the verge of convulsions because of the low salt.

Low salt is different from low potassium. With low potassium, a few days of high dosage will put you back where you should be, but not so with salt. It is a slow, slow process of ingesting the salt with your food. Took me nearly six weeks to get my salt level back to normal, but I have and I continue to thank the Lord. I am slowly improving. It is a slow process of up for a while then back but my ups are getting higher and longer and the lows are not as low as they had been.

115

We talk a lot about loving the sinner but hating the sin. Just how can anyone do such a thing? We have discussed this often in our Sunday School and Bible classes. It has always sounded good and proper until you come face to face with the actual facts. I woke up a few days ago with the clearest memory of a dream about that very thing. I saw myself walking along a street, unpaved and no sidewalks. As I was passing a larger business type building, someone called me "Come in." As I walked in, I saw several men and women gathered around a meeting table. I sensed these were the governing people of the city. Before I could say anything, they held out a small card and asked if I would give this card to Librarian at her house. I agreed as it was on my way. I walked on through a small town filled with beautiful flowers everywhere. Most of them were blue, but there were others of every possible color. The sun was so bright and not a cloud to be seen.

Librarian's house was near. I could see it, and it was cute, rickety, little, brightly painted house in a cartoonish looking way. A little rickety walking bridge crossed a clear little creek to the path that led to the rickety little porch. I just walked up to the door and walked on in with the intentions of laying the card on her table, but I was very surprised to see three young girls. I asked them what they were doing there. They weren't put out in the least. They were "Reading her books, but must go home for supper." One was the tallest with coal black hair. On her left was the red-haired one, and on her right was the smallest with long blonde braids. As I watched them leave, Librarian walked in. She read the card she had picked up from the table and tears came to her eyes. I had become just an onlooker.

Carpenter came in just then and put his arms around her and asked what was wrong. I knew they were talking about the card and that the card said they were living in sin, living together but unmarried and to please end it because of the effect on the young people in the community. Carpenter left for his work, and Librarian was about to do the same. She stepped out onto the porch and saw a neighbor coming down the street with a large plastic tub of water and clothes. He saw that Librarians rickety porch railing was on fire. He immediately went and poured the water, clothes and all, on the fire. Librarian spoke bitterly

116

"Don't bother. We're sinners. Why would you help us?" "But you are our neighbor, and we care about you." The rest of the neighbors soon were gathered around with more water to stop the fire, food for everyone to eat, lumber and supplies to repair the rail and anything else they might need.

The next scene I saw was the little blonde girl and her mother. The mother was brushing the girl's hair, and the little blonde asked her mother, "Why did everyone give them all that stuff when they are doing something wrong?" And the mother said, "Darling, we don't hate our Librarian and Carpenter. We do hate the sin. We know they are doing wrong but we continue to love them and pray that they will soon begin to live differently. Yes, we love our Librarian and Carpenter."

One of our neighbors to the north of us was a poet-farmer, Bill Yeats. Bill lived alone on the farm, so his wife and daughters could live in town for the girls to continue their schooling. Bill's house was on top of a small hill and had been destroyed by lightning strikes not just once but twice. Since we had all heard and believed that "lightning never hits twice in the same place," he had innocently replaced the house in that self-same spot after the first fire. I don't know why he did it the second time.

Anyway, he wrote a lot of poems about all the local people and gave Howard a copy of this poem he wrote about Howard and our horse named Bing. When Howard passed away, I inherited it. I cherish it for two reasons---Bill was an authentic Montana poet, and Howard was one of the last of the old-time Montana cowboys. And I got to know both of them.

Bill Yeats wrote a poem about Howard and Bing.
Taken shortly before WWII

BING AND HOWARD

Now if you all will listen,
A tale to you I'll bring,
A story of a cowboy,
and his famous horse named Bing.

Way out in old Montana,
Where the old Milk River flows,
Where the sun is always shining,
And the wind forever blows.

This cowboy's name was Howard,
He was lanky, tall and fair,
And when it came to taming broncs,
you bet that boy was there.

And Bing was sure a beauty,
Dark sorrel with black mane.
Like a gorgeous flame of color,
He would streak across the plain.

He was as nearly human as a horse could ever be,
He understood each word you'd say
and minded perfectly.

And when it came to roping steers,
Old Bing would never fail
to flop a husky four-year-old
and stand him on his tail.

But halter-breaking ornery colts
is where Old Bing does shine,
He'll yank them sideways off their pins
and drag them down the line.

One day, Carl Lee, the mailman,
who drove a model A,
Slipped down into a mud hole,
and there he had to stay.

Till Bing and Howard came along
A-looking for some fun,
Says Howard to Carl, "I'll pull you out."
Carl says, "It can't be done."

With his rope wrapped 'round the saddle-horn,
and tied back to the car, Howard says,
"Now Bing, let's take her out,
and show him who we are."

Then Bing began to haul and pull,
he did his best by heck!
But the saddle-cinch, it busted
and almost broke his neck.

Bing took his wind while they fixed the cinch,
then once more he did try.
Oh the saddle creaked,
and the old Ford squeaked,
but he took it out on high.

'Twas along in February in nineteen thirty-eight
when Howard jumped upon Bing's back
and went to see Bill Yeats.

He knew he would be welcome
for Bill lived all alone,
and thought it a treat, his friends to greet,
in his humble prairie home.

But Bill's place was no paradise,
as Old Bing quickly found
for on the old feed grinder
they made him go 'round and 'round.

They kept the poor chap busy,
Indeed, he earned his keep
for he packed the mail and cream cans,
thru snowdrifts belly deep.

And then one day a blizzard came,
A' sweeping o'er the plain,
which filled Bill's heart with worry
and drove him near insane.

For the barn was full of cattle
and the mow was full of air,
with not a spear of hay or straw
upon the floor boards bare.

But there was a little straw pile
off twenty rods or more,
with six big husky snowdrifts
'Tween it and the old barn door.

Bill says "We've got to have some straw,
at least a little bit,
but how to get it in the barn,
'tis a problem, I'll admit."

"I think my old tarpaulin
will work about the best."
"We'll pile a bunch of straw on that,
and Bing will do the rest."

So once more Old Bing saved the day,
and saved the cattle, too,
for he kept the mangers full of straw,
till once more skies were blue.

Oh, you will hear his praises sung
where ever cowboys meet,
for every day in every way,
Old Bing just can't be beat.

And when at last we gather
in the heavenly land so fair,
I'm sure we'll like it better

if we find Old Bing is there.

We always called Mom and Dad, Mama and Papa. The Crites kids called their parents mom and dad. I thought that was so sophisticated or something. Anyway, I was so anxious to grow up, so I could call my parents Mom and Dad. Uncle Frances and Aunt Flossie's family always used the mama and papa, too. They never got 'sophisticated', and kept right on with Mama and Papa even after they grew up. Apparently, they didn't share my feelings about it.

Another thing I was so naive about was the swearing. I have no idea why I knew it was wrong, at least for kids! That was another thing I was going to do when I grew up! Did I ever!!! When I think of it now, it makes me sick to my stomach.

I marvel that God is with me wherever I am and whatever I do. I have known "God is all around us all the time" since I was about 4 or 5 at least as long as I can remember. Ora, my sister, told me that. This is one of my oldest memories.

We were playing together, just the two of us. Floyd must have been too young to play outside with us. I don't know what caused her to tell me that. Maybe I was afraid of something, or maybe I was up to some mischief. I'm so glad she did tell me because that belief has never wavered. There were years when I had only that statement to carry with me, and it became a solid foundation to build on later.

I rode Bing out one evening to get the milk cows. It was a beautiful evening, so I let Bing pick his way as I was in no hurry. As I watched the sun getting low in the west I heard the dreaded sound of the prairie rattler! Then a whole chorus of them. I stopped daydreaming instantly and looked down. We were in the middle of a gopher town, and at the exit of each hole lay a rattler on alert. Bing apparently knew where each hoof was and so far, just got threats from the snakes! I sat frozen in the saddle, and it was only a few more steps before Bing had carried me safely out of town.

When a bunch of us got together, we almost always heard Dad say, "One kid is a good kid, two kids are half a kid, and three kids are no kid at all."

My college roommate, Marian, spent the weekend with me when I went home. She grew up in the Rockies, so she knew nothing about prairie rattlers. We went to visit Aunt Flossie and her family. As per usual, many other cousins were there, too. Two cousins were sent out on horseback to bring in the milk cows. About half a mile from the house, they saw a huge rattler, so one watched it while the other one rode back for reinforcements. Roy volunteered to kill it and brought it back to the house. It was unusually long and big for a prairie rattler. Roy was at least six feet tall. He held the snake by the tail and let it hang straight down. The head touched the ground while Roy held his arm straight out from his shoulder.

Marian decided she wanted the snakeskin, so the boys obligingly skinned it and gave it to her. She filled it full of dirt, and we headed back to the dorm. We arrived after lights out, so no one saw us. Marian laid a newspaper on the floor between our beds, coiled the snake skin on it, and we got a good night's sleep. When the buzzer woke us up in the morning, we lay still and waited as one friend after another pulled open the door to wake us, saw the snake, screamed and slammed the door and left. Marion kept this right there until it began to smell bad, before she finally decided to give it up and dumped it in the garbage.

One time, I got to go with Dad when he made a fast trip to a neighbor's. I have no idea how it happened that I alone got to go along. When we arrived at the neighbors, I went off to play with the kids, I was having a lot of fun until all at once I realized Dad was gone, and I was still there. I want behind one of the buildings and started crying. They all came around me and tried to encourage me, but all I remember is peeking around the corner and still no Dad. I have no idea how long it took him to remember and come back. My memory of the incident ended at that time.

About the dumbest game that we ever played was one that I only remember playing with Floyd. He was four years younger than I and I was seven or eight, I guess. The game rules were take a handful of the other guy's hair at the same time he took hold of yours then pull until one called it off. I can't remember either of us ever calling it quits, but I do remember hearing a pop from Floyd's scalp that scared me half to death. I was sure I was scalping him. I let go as fast as I could. We never told anyone, and he never seemed to have any bad effects, but I can't remember ever playing that game again.

Ora and I used to play house. It was a dry year, but we were making mud pies and the whole bit when I decided to do some 'canning'. I got a jar and filled the jar with the only thing growing nearby, Russian thistles. After filling it on up with water, I put the lid back on and set it on the shelf (Actually a box laying on its' side. We had good imaginations!) We got called into the house, so it was probably a week later of hot weather before I checked on my 'canning'. I opened it up, and it really smelled bad, but I just **had** to taste it. I put a little bit on my tongue, and I can still taste that horrible taste. There is no way to describe that taste. It wasn't sour or bitter but a combination of all bad tastes you can imagine. That has to be over eighty years ago.

There are so many reasons to believe that the Bible is truth and light.

1. There are more copies of it than any other single ancient manuscript.
2. There are more mentions of it in other manuscripts than any other, over 2,500 in fact that have been found so far.
3. It has never been proven false. Names of cities and people mentioned only in the Bible keep coming to light in archaeological digs.
4. It was written over a period of 400 years by men who never knew each other but still agreed on all major points.
5. The grammar used was proper. It did not have to have humans correct it.
6. Believing it can change the meanest, nastiest, most hateful person into a saint.
7. It can take the most cowardly and turn him/her into a strong, brave person.

I could go on and on, but whole books have been written about this and better written than I can. I advise you to check into it if you think the Bible is just a myth. The person who reads the Bible and starts living by it **is changed**. I know this from my own personal experience. I look back and compare the meaning of the first 48 years of my life with the last 42 or 3, and I am amazed! I never knew real love. My love for my husband and my children changed so much for the better. Becoming a practicing Christian changed my whole life completely. I have seen God answer prayer after prayer. Very little of it has to do with 'things', although he has taken care of that, too, and I trust Him to continue. This is the time we realized the importance of tithing. God gives us everything we have and all he asks is that one tenth of it go to His work, helping others less fortunate than we and to tell others about Him. When we really settled into the routine of true tithing, we found how faithfully God stretched the other ninety percent to take care of all we needed.

When one starts looking for one's life partner, there are so many things to look for. These can be shortened to a few that include the small items that still need to be handled after marriage and for a lifetime. No matter how perfect he or she seems before the wedding, there will be faults that show up later. First of all, can you talk together? Can you safely confide in each other knowing this conversation will not come up in the community's casual conversation? Do you like each other? Do you have the same ideals? Do you have the same attitude toward money? Do you both want a big family or just one or two children? Do both of you take pride in your and your spouse's jobs? If you women plan to be stay-at-home moms, be sure your chosen appreciates the great stress and work required. Make sure you choose a spouse willing to help anytime help is needed. This is for both men and women. Do you admire each other? This is not just a physical attraction. Included here, and much more important, are the integrity, the love of his or her work and the will to do it well. Don't forget honesty and truth, also consideration for one another. Each one must protect the other's ego and back. Are you both determined to make this last for your lifetime? There will be times when you will be tempted to sell your spouse for a nickel. These are the times when the correct answers to all the above questions will really count. I know a couple who said when they got married----He: If you get fat like your mother, I'll divorce you. She: If you get bald like your Dad, I'll divorce you. Thirty years later, she was fat, and he was bald, but they had realized those were not the important things in life and were still a happily married couple.

We were living north of Gildford when we cousins walked out to the pasture to bring in the milk cows. We were at the west end of the pasture, about a mile from the house when we saw a skunk. Skunks are not good. They liked chicken dinners as well as we did, so we immediately decided this critter had to go. It had met its Waterloo.

Now this was real prairie, no tree branches laying around to be used as weapons to hasten his demise. Of course, we never carried a .22 along when doing chores. The only weapons that were handy were rocks! We had plenty of them, so the sentence came down, "death by stoning!" We made a point of not getting behind him when he sprayed!

We never once thought about the fact that although his spray never hit us directly, it settled slowly down on all the grass. So a nice big circle was covered and inside that circle lay our supply of stones. The grass was probably 6 to 10 inches tall, well over our shoes. We also had to bend over to retrieve our ammo, so our hands were saturated, too. After circling and stoning for 15 to 20 minutes we had killed the poor thing. The wind came out of the west, so by the time we got home, the odor had gotten there well ahead of us. The horrible stench was there, and no explanations were needed as we reinforced the odor.

How things have changed for ordering from the catalog. When I was a child, we had a couple of rules; we should write legibly on the order blank that comes with the catalog. Some catalogs included several blank order sheets. First, you listed all the wanted items including the weight and cost and then how many, then we added the columns. We figured in needed postage with the order cost, placed the filled order blank plus the correct amount of money in the envelope and sealed it tightly. If it was before 10:20 a.m. it was possible to meet the mail carrier on his route, and you could set your clock by him or her.

Six to eight days later, the items ordered were in your mailbox. Occasionally, all shipping connections worked perfectly, so we got our order in 5 days - Monday to Friday. Mail was delivered Monday, Wednesday and Friday. The mail carrier's motto meant something then. They did deliver in all kinds of weather, and we had a lot of winters with very, very deep snow, and they had ingenious ways of combating the weather and the roads.

There were no snow plows in those days. You had to use your shovel when you got stuck. All farmers had one or more milk cows, so they could separate the milk and ship the excess cream to the creamery. We lived north of the main Great Northern Railroad line where the towns were located approximately 6 miles apart. Our cream traveled by U.S. mail to Hingham or Gildford where it was put on the train to Havre and a few days later, the empty can and the check came back by the mail. Excess separated milk was fed to the milk cows calves or to hogs. The recalcitrant child was told, not always in a joking way, "We should have knocked you in the head when you were born and fed the milk to the pigs."

GOD BLESS CARL AND ELMER
By William Yates

To the farmers and stock growers of Montana's bleak prairie,
The winter of '36 and '37 was filled with misery.
For it started in November, a throwing down the snow.
While almost steady day and night, the old north wind did blow.
Soon the highways and the byways, with drifts were all snow bound
Til even with a saddle horse, you could hardly get around.
Day after day the same old thing, blizzards and steady cold.
People were running out of grub, coal piles were getting low,
While the haystacks and straw piles, looked awful small, you know.
Now in the town of Gildford. Where the muddy Sage Creek flows,
There dwelt Carl Lee the mail man, whom everybody knows.
Yes, Carl Lee had the contract, to haul the US mail
From Gildford out to Fairchild, on the old Milk River trail.
Now when it came to hauling mail, you bet Carl knew "his stuff".
For he'd made many, many trips when road were fierce and tough.
But people were all sure that Carl, had met his Waterloo.
No car nor horse could buck those drifts,
and they wondered what he'd do.
But Carl just grinned from ear to ear, while his manly chest did swell.
As he said, "Now folks you know the mail
goes through in spite of hades."
He called on Elmer Jorgensen, and thus to him did say,
"Your Caterpillar tractor, I'm sure will save the day."
"It has a cab that's good and tight, with a heater in it too."
So, it matters not how tough it gets, I know that we'll get through."
Then both of them got busy, went to work with might and main.
And soon rigged up an outfit, that took them straight to fame.
They built a dog house on a sleigh, with a door and cute window.
Set a stove inside to keep it warm, when the mercury was low
Next, they built a great big rack, upon a husky sleigh,
Hooked those up to the tractor, to haul out coal and hay.

Then early in the morning, on a cold and winter day,
They started out for Fairchild, just 30 miles away.
When the farmers saw that outfit, their hearts were filled with cheer,
For with Carl and Elmer on the job, there was nothing more for fear.
They brought them coal and groceries, as well as feed and hay,
Also, the mail and parcels, from loved ones far away.
But steadily those mighty drifts, wider and higher grew.
While day and night the old north wind, louder and fiercer blew.
They did their worst but could not stop, this brave and dauntless pair.
With hearts of steel, that never knew, the meaning of despair.
So, hour after hour, mile after mile, steady the whole day long,
That faithful and loyal Cat purred forth it's cheering song.
Through the drifting snow and piercing
wind, ever ready and willing to go,
Slowly but surely it made its way, ore the billows of drifted snow.
While people all both big and small, along the old mail route,
prayed God to protect the whole outfit, with hearts that were devout.
Yes, God bless Carl and Elmer, and that sturdy little Cat,
Sure, their fame will live forever, you can bet your life on that.

I know it's true, and most people believe God is present with each of us no matter where we go or what we're doing. Of course, He is unhappy with some of our actions, but He did not make a multitude of robots. He made us to be intelligent, thinking, loving humans with a will to make decisions. He gave us love, and He especially honored us by giving us the ability to join Him in creating new humans. He gave us the special love we need for these new human creations, enough love to carry us through the years of caring and training for these new humans.

Caring for and training these new humans is truly a full-time job. Having one point seven babies per family is the style nowadays. If they are 5 or 6 years apart, it's like being an only child. Of course, there are monetary advantages, but that is no true compensation for having to grow up the lone girl or boy in the family.

Naturally, siblings will have arguments and disagreements, but if you love and raise them in the true love that God alone can give, they will outgrow this. The best way to raise children is to praise them when they really do a good job. It doesn't hurt them if you gently and lovingly correct them. Show them the correct way, and they will live that way. Let them help and show them the correct way to do a thing, and once they do it correctly, then praise them. Too much praise and too much scolding are both bad for the child. They need to respect a day's hard work and realize people need to do it to be truly happy.

Anyone who finds a life-work that also includes the person's idea of enjoying the day is truly blessed. Raising and training a child is the job of both parents for both boys and girls. The girls need fathers who are loving, caring, and helping, so they will never be satisfied with a man who is not good husband material. The girls need their mothers to help them learn how to be a real woman who is a model for her in every way. Fathers need to respect the hard work that every mother performs, and the mother needs to respect the hard work every father does, when both are home with the children, they need to share all responsibilities required of both. A good true real father or husband does not come home from work go in to the TV and spend the rest of his time at home there. His family needs to come before the latest football game or a movie.

Most people believe God made the earth, made everything, the stars, planets, even space. He made the Earth and all the Seas, mountains, plains, plants, sea animals and last of all, He made humans. Still, when it comes to believing Mary was a virgin before and after Jesus's birth, they really don't believe that God could do that without a man's help. Duh! if God could say, "Let there be light", and there was light, why is it so hard to believe He said, "Let a baby grow inside Mary's womb," and it happened just like that?

AT NINETY

Today, dear Lord, I'm 90 and there's so much I haven't done,
I hope, dear Lord, you'll let me live until I'm 91.
But then, if I haven't finished all I want to do,
Would you let me stay awhile, until I'm 92?

So many places I want to go, so very much to see,
Do you think that you could manage to make it 93?
The world is changing very fast. There is so much in store.
I'd like it very much to live to 94.

And if by then I'm still alive, I'd like to stay till 95.
More planes will be in the air, so I'd really like to stick
And see what happens to the world when I'm 96.
I know, dear Lord, it's so much to ask (and it must be nice in Heaven),
But I would really like to stay until I'm 97.

I know by then I won't be fast, and sometimes will be late,
But it would be so pleasant to be around at 98.
I will have seen so many things, and had a wonderful time,
So I'm sure that I'll be willing to leave at 99!

MAYBE!!!!!!!!

Descendants of Frank Revilo Huestis

Generation 1

1. **FRANK REVILO HUESTIS** was born in 1855. He died in 1932. He married IDA ALICE BROWN. She was born in 1867. She died in 1944.

Frank Revilo Huestis and Ida Alice Brown had the following children:

    i.   ORRIE ETHEL HUESTIS was born in 1887. She died in 1929. She married FRANCIS ADELBERT SMITH. He was born in 1869. He died in 1943.

    ii.   FRANCIS EDWIN HUESTIS was born in 1889. He died in 1953. He married FLORENCE OLIVE SMITH. She was born in 1894. She died in 1974.

    iii.   FLORENCE ELMA HUESTIS was born in 1894. She died in 1980. She married DAKOTA TERRITORY SMITH. He was born in 1883. He died in 1955.

    iv.   ACHSAH IDA HUESTIS was born in 1899. She died in 1982. She married FRED CRITES. He was born in 1896. He died in 1961.

v. MARIAN JEAN HUESTIS was born in 1907. She died in 1986. She married JOHN ALLOYOUS CHVILICEK. He was born in 1901. He died in 1959.

GENERATION 2

2. **ORRIE ETHEL HUESTIS** (Frank Revilo) was born in 1887. She died in 1929. She married FRANCIS ADELBERT SMITH. He was born in 1869. He died in 1943.

Francis Adelbert Smith and Orrie Ethel Huestis had the following children:

i. LEE FRANCIS SMITH was born in 1904. He died in 1974. He married ELLA LILLIAN ELMER. She was born in 1910.

ii. DESSIE ETHEL SMITH was born in 1905. She died in 1926. She married RALPH ERNEST SHIPMAN. He was born in 1895. He died in 1975.

iii. GEORGE ADELBERT SMITH was born in 1907. He died in 1967. He married MARIE (AKA NETTIE) ANTOINETTE SHARPLES. She was born in 1907. She died in 1986.

iv. CHARLES REVILO HOWARD SMITH was born in 1908. He died in 1992.

v. LULA MILDRED SMITH was born in 1910. She died in 1977. She married KENNETH EDWIN SHAFER. He was born in 1909. He died in 1976.

vi. ALICE LARENA SMITH was born in 1912. She died in 1993. She married LAVERN JOHN ERNEST CONNOR. He was born in 1912. He died in 1989.

vii. VELMA ACHSAH SMITH was born in 1914. She died in 1936. She married ALFRED HOWARD JOHNSON. He was born in 1911. He died in 1963.

viii. VERA MARGARET SMITH was born in 1917. She died in 1927.

ix. LENA MARIE SMITH was born in 1919. She died in 1920.

x. LEONA MARIAN SMITH was born in 1919. She died in 1920.

xi. ORRIE IRENE SMITH was born in 1921. She died in 2004. She married MONTE THOMAS HEWITT. He was born in 1919. He died in 2004.

xii. LUCILLE MAE SMITH was born on 04 Apr 1924 in Farm north of Hingham, Hill County, Montana. She married HARRY THOMAS JENSEN on 25 Dec 1945 in Zion Lutheran Church, Glendive, Dawson Co, MT. He was born on 21 Feb 1920. He died on 06 May 2010.

xiii. FLOYD HAROLD SMITH was born in 1928. He died in 1999. He married (1) JUANITA ANN WALL. She was born in 1934. She died in 1983. He married (2) SANDRA L. DICKMAN MCDONALD. She was born in 1947.

3. **FRANCIS EDWIN HUESTIS** (Frank Revilo) was born in 1889. He died in 1953. He married FLORENCE OLIVE SMITH. She was born in 1894. She died in 1974.

Francis Edwin Huestis and Florence Olive Smith had the following children:

i. BERNICE ALICE HUESTIS was born in 1913. She died in 2000. She married MARION STREETER. He was born in 1911.

ii. MILDRED LILLIAN HUESTIS was born in 1914. She married GORDON THOMAS OBIE. He was born in 1917.

iii. DELILAH MAXINE HUESTIS was born in 1917. She married (1) EDWARD TANGMO. She married (2) LAURANCE MORD.

iv. INEZ LUCILLE HUESTIS was born in 1920. She married WINFRED PAUL HALTER JR. He was born in 1923.

v. FRANK EMMETT HUESTIS was born in 1922. He married MARGARET ELLEN WALKER. She was born in 1925.

vi. LEONA JEAN HUESTIS was born in 1925. She died in 2008. She married LOUIS JOSEPH FALTRINO. He was born in 1925. He died in 1994.

vii. LEROY LEE HUESTIS was born in 1927. He died in 1968. He married BETTY JEAN PLUMMER. She was born in 1928. She died in 1968.

viii. EVELYN JOY HUESTIS was born in 1929. She died in 2004. She married WILLIAM PURKETT. He was born in 1928.

ix. GAY YVONNE HUESTIS was born in 1933. She died in 1990. She married DONALD OSCAR DAHLBERG. He was born in 1930.

4. **FLORENCE ELMA HUESTIS** (Frank Revilo) was born in 1894. She died in 1980. She married DAKOTA TERRITORY SMITH. He was born in 1883. He died in 1955.

Dakota Territory Smith and Florence Elma Huestis had the following children:

i. DAKOTA THEODORE SMITH was born in 1912. He died in 1982. He married GUINEVERE HUNTER. She was born in 1914.

ii. MARVIN REVILO SMITH was born in 1912. He died in 1962. He married GLADY R.PATRICK. She was born in 1912.

iii. DOROTHY FLORENCE SMITH was born in 1914. She married EPHRIAM JUSTIN LEE. He was born in 1901. He died in 1975.

iv. DORA ETTA SMITH was born in 1916. She married HARRY LARS ANDERSON. He was born in 1909. He died in 1989.

v. HAZEL MAY SMITH was born in 1919. She married MERRILL MURTON ZIMMERMAN.

vi. ROBERT ROY SMITH was born in 1921. He married BETTY ARLENE PEDERSON. She was born in 1924. She died in 1985.

vii. RICHARD ORVAL SMITH was born in 1925. He married (1) LAURA BURBRIDGE MOSSIER. He married (2) SHIRLEY WHEELER.

5. **ACHSAH IDA HUESTIS** (Frank Revilo) was born in 1899. She died in 1982. She married FRED CRITES. He was born in 1896. He died in 1961.

Fred Crites and Achsah Ida Huestis had the following children:

i. VERN IRWIN3 CRITES was born in 1919. He died in 1997. He married ALBERTA MAE STREETER. She was born in 1918.

ii. CLEONA MARIAN CRITES was born in 1921. She died in 1983. She married CARLTON EARL POORE. He was born in 1907. He died in 1984.

iii. DONALD FRANCIS CRITES was born in 1922. He died in 1972. He married (1) IONE PANGBORN. She was born in 1918. He married (2) MILDRED PANGBORN BROWN.

iv. HAROLD HOLLIS CRITES was born in 1923. He died in 2004. He married (1) JOAN ELLENORE MAY. He married (2) OPAL LORRAINE FISHER. She was born in 1924. He married (3) SHEILA M COUTURE. She was born in 1939.

v. GRACE MARIE CRITES was born in 1924. She died in 1924.

vi. FRED VERN CRITES JR. was born in 1925. He died in 1926.

vii. LOIS LORRAINE CRITES was born in 1927. She died in 2009. She married LLOYD AMOS OLSON. He was born in 1925.

viii.DOROTHY JEAN CRITES was born in 1930. She married ALLAN JAMES KIDD. He was born in 1925. He died in 2005.

ix. DORENE VALARY CRITES was born in 1931. She died in 2010. She married EUGENE CONARD RUTTER. He was born in 1921. He died in 1995.

x. LARENA CRITES was born in 1932. She married GORDON LYLE STEWART. He was born in 1929. He died in 1998.

xi. JUNE ARLENE CRITES was born in 1934. She died in 2009. She married JR. HARRY YOUSO. He was born in 1929.

xii. RICHARD MELVIN CRITES was born in 1937. He died in 2000. He married (1) DOROTHY MAY PRICE. He married (2) DORINE MAY DICKENSON. She was born in 1933.

xiii.WARREN FAYET CRITES was born in 1940. He died in 1941.

xiv. JEANNE RAE CRITES was born in 1942. She married JOE LLOYD JOHNSTON. He was born in 1940.

6. **MARIAN JEAN HUESTIS** (Frank Revilo) was born in 1907. She died in 1986. She married JOHN ALLOYOUS CHVILICEK. He was born in 1901. He died in 1959.

John Alloyous Chvilicek and Marian Jean Huestis had the following children:

    i.   JOHN EDWARD3 CHVILICEK was born in 1927. He died in 1987. He married STELLA KIRKULIET.

    ii. JAMES ALFRED CHVILICEK was born in 1929. He died in 1987. He married CHARLOTTE LORRAINE MEADOWS. She was born in 1930.

    iii. LEONARD GLENRO CHVILICEK was born in 1930. He died in 1993. He married LOY ANN PATRICK. She was born in 1941.

    iv. NORBERT FRANCIS ALVIN CHVILICEK was born in 1932. He died in 1995. He married BERTHA LORRAINE CADY. She was born in 1940.

    v. LAWRENCE EUGENE CHVILICEK was born in 1934. He married CAROLE ANN STORY. She was born in 1939.

    vi. ALICE CAMILLE CHVILICEK was born in 1936. She died in 2005. She married ARNOLD FRANCIS LANGEL. He was born in 1930. He died in 1966.

    vii. ROBERT NOLAN CHVILICEK was born in 1937. He married BARBARA JEAN OPHUS.

    viii. GERALD ANTHONY CHVILICEK was born in 1943. He died in 1999.

Generation 3

7. **LEE FRANCIS SMITH** (Orrie Ethel Huestis, Frank Revilo Huestis) was born in 1904. He died in 1974. He married ELLA LILLIAN ELMER. She was born in 1910.

Lee Francis Smith and Ella Lillian Elmer had the following child:

    i.   THERESA BETTY4 SMITH was born in 1944. She married JORDAN WHEAT LAMBERT IV. He was born in 1924. He died in 1990.

8. **DESSIE ETHEL SMITH** (Orrie Ethel Huestis, Frank Revilo Huestis) was born in 1905. She died in 1926. She married RALPH ERNEST SHIPMAN. He was born in 1895. He died in 1975.

Ralph Ernest Shipman and Dessie Ethel Smith had the following child:

    i.   ERNEST RALPH4 SHIPMAN was born in 1925. He married BERNICE LORRAINE EWY. She was born in 1928. She died in 1972.

9. **GEORGE ADELBERT SMITH** (Orrie Ethel Huestis, Frank Revilo Huestis) was born in 1907. He died in 1967. He married MARIE (AKA NETTIE) ANTOINETTE SHARPLES. She was born in 1907. She died in 1986.

George Adelbert Smith and Marie (aka Nettie) Antoinette Sharples had the following children:

    i.   MERLYN JUDSON4 SMITH was born in 1934. He married (1) BEVERLY JEAN MILLER. She was born in 1932. She died on 20 May 2003. He married (2) JOANIE MATLACK. She was born in 1934.

ii. GEORGE ANTHONY SMITH was born in 1936. He died in 2011. He married (1) WILLA LEE GRIFFITH. She was born in 1939. He married (2) MURIEL ELIZABETH PARKINSON. She was born in 1935. She died in 2009.

10. LULA MILDRED SMITH (Orrie Ethel Huestis, Frank Revilo Huestis) was born in 1910. She died in 1977. She married KENNETH EDWIN SHAFER. He was born in 1909. He died in 1976.

Kenneth Edwin Shafer and Lula Mildred Smith had the following children:

i. RITA MAE SHAFER was born in 1934. She married CHARLES B. MOORE. He was born in 1930. He died in 2004.

ii. VERA ETHEL SHAFER was born in 1937. She married JAMES S. MONTGOMERY. He was born in 1937.

iii. KEITH GORDON SHAFER was born in 1938. He married SHARON YVONNE JOHNSON. She was born in 1939. She died in 2015.

iv. VERLYN GLENN SHAFER was born in 1940. He died in 2009. He married JOANNE E. BRUIER. She died in 2003.

v. NEAL EUGENE SHAFER was born in 1946. He married CHARLENE ERWAY.

vi. GREG ALLEN SHAFER was born in 1949. He died in 2016. He married JUDY STORMSHAK.

vii. RONALD ROY SHAFER was born in 1952. He died in 1964.

11. ALICE LARENA SMITH (Orrie Ethel Huestis, Frank Revilo Huestis) was born in 1912. She died in 1993. She married LAVERN JOHN ERNEST CONNOR. He was born in 1912. He died in 1989.

Lavern John Ernest Connor and Alice LaRena Smith had the following children:

    i.   HAROLD ERNEST4 CONNOR was born in 1934. He died in 1937.

    ii.   LAVERN LYLE CONNOR was born in 1938. He married ANDREA SCHLAB. She was born in 1939.

    iii.   BERNARD JOHN CONNOR was born in 1939. He married (1) SHARON HAGGERTY. She was born in 1939. He married (2) BARBARA SATHER. She was born in 1950.

    iv.   DOROTHY JEAN CONNOR was born in 1940. She married DONALD STAFFORD. He was born in 1939.

12. VELMA ACHSAH SMITH (Orrie Ethel Huestis, Frank Revilo Huestis) was born in 1914. She died in 1936. She married ALFRED HOWARD JOHNSON. He was born in 1911. He died in 1963.

Alfred Howard Johnson and Velma Achsah Smith had the following child:

    i.   MARLENE ANN4 JOHNSON was born in 1935. She married EDWIN C. HANSON. He was born in 1935.

13. ORRIE IRENE SMITH (Orrie Ethel Huestis, Frank Revilo Huestis) was born in 1921. She died in 2004. She married MONTE THOMAS HEWITT. He was born in 1919. He died in 2004.

Monte Thomas Hewitt and Orrie Irene Smith had the following children:

    i.   SANDRA KAY4 HEWITT was born in 1944. She married (1) JOSEPH THOMAS MULDOON. She married (2) GLENN SIDNEY RITTENHOUSE. He was born in 1924.

    ii.   MONTE RUSSELL HEWITT was born in 1945. He married (1) SHIELA MOULTON. He married (2) VIVIAN ANN CLARK BARKER.

    iii.   THOMAS WILLIAM HEWITT was born in 1951. He married CATHLEEN MAY CASEY. She was born in 1953.

    iv.   NINA JEAN HEWITT was born in 1955. She married FORREST GRAVES. He was born in 1952.

    v.   LYNNE ANN HEWITT was born in 1956. She married (1) RONALD GAIL CIMMER. She married (2) JAY JOHNSON. He was born in 1956.

14. LUCILLE MAE SMITH (Orrie Ethel Huestis, Frank Revilo Huestis) was born on 04 Apr 1924 in Farm north of Hingham, HillCounty, Montana. She married HARRY THOMAS JENSEN on 25 Dec 1945 in Zion LutheranChurch, Glendive, Dawson Co, MT. He was born on 21 Feb 1920. He died on 06 May 2010.

Harry Thomas Jensen and Lucille (750652) Mae Smith had the following children:

i. MAE EVA4 JENSEN was born on 22 Dec 1946 in Glendive, Montana. She married JIMMIE DAVID RITTAL on 02 Sep 1967 in Circle, McCone, Montana, USA. He was born on 19 Dec 1941 in Circle, Montana.

ii. TERRY SOREN JENSEN was born on 04 Dec 1948 in Glendive, Dawson, Montana, USA. He married BARBARA ELAINE SUKUT on 17 Dec 1969 in Glendive, Dawson, Montana, USA. She was born on 01 Nov 1949 in Billings, Yellowstone, Montana, USA.

iii. DEBRA ANN JENSEN was born on 29 Nov 1949 in Terry, Prairie, Montana, USA. She married DONALD ALLAN KLEPPELID on 17 Jun 1972 in Circle, McCone, Montana, USA. He was born on 27 Dec 1951 in Circle, McCone, Montana, USA.

iv. DAVID THOMAS JENSEN was born on 06 Mar 1951 in Miles City, Custer, Montana, USA. He married MARY LYNN GEER on 09 Jun 1973 in Circle, McCone, Montana, USA. She was born on 29 Dec 1955 in Wolf Point, Roosevelt, Montana, USA.

15. FLOYD HAROLD SMITH (Orrie Ethel Huestis, Frank Revilo Huestis) was born in 1928. He died in 1999. He married (1) JUANITA ANN WALL. She was born in 1934. She died in 1983. He married (2) SANDRA L. DICKMAN MCDONALD. She was born in 1947.

Floyd Harold Smith and Juanita Ann Wall had the following children:

i. LIBBY DIANNE4 SMITH was born in 1954. She married (1) DAVID ALAN SHRINER. He was born in 1942. He died in 1981. She married (2) QUENT COLVIN.

ii. RORY DOUGLAS SMITH was born in 1956. He married ROSE MARY WALSTON. She was born in 1957.

iii. TRACY CHRISTINE SMITH was born in 1957. She married JAMES CONNER. He was born in 1952.

16. BERNICE ALICE HUESTIS (Francis Edwin, Frank Revilo) was born in 1913. She died in 2000. She married MARION STREETER. He was born in 1911.

Marion Streeter and Bernice Alice Huestis had the following children:

i. DELORES MAY4 STREETER was born in 1934. She married ROLAND MORD. He was born in 1926.

ii. BERT EDWIN STREETER was born in 1935. He married (1) JOANN MILLER. He married (2) MARY MURL ALEXANDER. She was born in 1948.

iii. SHARON LEE STREETER was born in 1937. She married DONALD LEE JENKINS. He was born in 1940.

iv. MARIN MARK STREETER was born in 1951. He married PEGGY LYNN JOHNSON. She was born in 1953.

17. MILDRED LILLIAN HUESTIS (Francis Edwin, Frank Revilo) was born in 1914. She married GORDON THOMAS OBIE. He was born in 1917.

Gordon Thomas Obie and Mildred Lillian Huestis had the following children:

i. GARY GAIL4 OBIE was born in 1938. He married MARY LINDSETH.

ii. BARRY BRIAN OBIE was born in 1941. He married BETTY POWELL.

iii. FLORENCE ANN OBIE was born in 1942. She died in 1983. She married NOLAN EDWIN SCHEID.

18. INEZ LUCILLE HUESTIS (Francis Edwin, Frank Revilo) was born in 1920. She married WINFRED PAUL HALTER JR. He was born in 1923.

Winfred Paul Halter Jr and Inez Lucille Huestis had the following children:

i. ELDONNA EDITH4 HALTER was born in 1943. She married LOREN ALVIN JENKINS. He was born in 1941.

ii. CAROLYN JOYCE HALTER was born in 1948. She married C. STEPHEN NORRIS. He was born in 1943.

iii. WINFRED PAUL HALTER III was born in 1949. He married RENEE TILLICEE JURENKA. She was born in 1948.

iv. JOEY ANN HALTER was born in 1950. She married (1) TOM UDELHOVEN. She married (2) ROBERT SILVERNALE. She married (3) HARLEY HETTICK. He was born in 1942.

v. JACKSON THOMAS HALTER was born in 1954. He married LESLIE TRAINER.

vi. GAY CHERRI HALTER was born in 1956. She married RONALD ARNFRED PEARSON. He was born in 1954.

19. FRANK EMMETT HUESTIS (Francis Edwin, Frank Revilo) was born in 1922. He married MARGARET ELLEN WALKER. She was born in 1925.

Frank Emmett Huestis and Margaret Ellen Walker had the following children:

   i.   LELAND LEROY4 HUESTIS was born in 1945. He died in 1977. He married ARDIS JOWAYNE SCHMIDT. She was born in 1943.

   ii. LANA LEE HUESTIS was born in 1947. She married (1) MICHAEL FRAZIER. She married (2) JERRY LARSON. He was born in 1947.

   iii. GLEN ALAN HUESTIS was born in 1950. He married LAURIE NORDRUM. She was born in 1952.

   iv. LARRY GENE HUESTIS was born in 1951. He married KIMBERLY REYNOLDS. She was born in 1955.

   v.   RAY IRVIN HUESTIS was born in 1954. He married PEGGY REINOWSKI. She was born in 1952.

20. LEONA JEAN HUESTIS (Francis Edwin, Frank Revilo) was born in 1925. She died in 2008. She married LOUIS JOSEPH FALTRINO. He was born in 1925. He died in 1994.

Louis Joseph Faltrino and Leona Jean Huestis had the following children:

   i.   TANA RAI4 FALTRINO was born in 1947.

   ii. DEAN DWAIN FALTRINO was born in 1955. He married CATHERINE ANN RICHARDSON. She was born in 1958.

iii. CARRIE FRANCES FALTRINO was born in 1959. She married LARRY CARLSON. He was born in 1957.

21. LEROY LEE HUESTIS (Francis Edwin, Frank Revilo) was born in 1927. He died in 1968. He married BETTY JEAN PLUMMER. She was born in 1928. She died in 1968.

Leroy Lee Huestis and Betty Jean Plummer had the following children:

i. DIANNA LYNN4 HUESTIS was born in 1947. She married ROBERT JAMES MONTALBETTI. He was born in 1945.

ii. RONALD LEE HUESTIS was born in 1949. He died in 1974. He married KRIS LEGERE.

iii. BONNIE JEAN HUESTIS was born in 1950. She married (1) GARY ROBERTSON. She married (2) DENNIS FREY. He was born in 1945.

iv. PEGGY LEE HUESTIS was born in 1953.

v. MARY MILDRED HUESTIS was born in 1955. She married DARROLD HUTCHINSON. He was born in 1951.

vi. DEBORAH ANN HUESTIS was born in 1959. She died in 2015. She married JERRY ANDERSON. He was born in 1962.

vii. CINDY LOU HUESTIS was born in 1961. She married STEPHEN KEASTER.

22. EVELYN JOY HUESTIS (Francis Edwin, Frank Revilo) was born in 1929. She died in 2004. She married WILLIAM PURKETT. He was born in 1928.

William Purkett and Evelyn Joy Huestis had the following children:

i. WILLIAM EDWIN PURKETT was born in 1949. He died in 2000. He married MARJORIE MEIKAMP. She was born in 1943.

ii. SHARON KATHERINE PURKETT was born in 1950. She married (1) RICHARD WILLIAM NORSTROM. He was born in 1949. She married (2) RICHARD EDWARD LARSON. He was born in 1947.

iii. GAYLE MARIE PURKETT was born in 1952. She married DOUGLAS WAYNE JENKINS. He was born in 1952.

iv. ARLA KAY PURKETT was born in 1954. She married EDWIN JOHN KEELING. He was born in 1952.

v. NARDA LYNN PURKETT was born in 1955. She married WARREN ANDERSON. He was born in 1935.

23. GAY YVONNE HUESTIS (Francis Edwin, Frank Revilo) was born in 1933. She died in 1990. She married DONALD OSCAR DAHLBERG. He was born in 1930.

Donald Oscar Dahlberg and Gay Yvonne Huestis had the following children:

i. DONNA GAYLE DAHLBERG was born in 1951. She married STEPHEN PETER DETHMAN. He was born in 1950.

ii. JAMES DONALD DAHLBERG was born in 1962.

iii. LORI GAY DAHLBERG was born in 1964. She married CURRY KIM. He was born in 1962.

iv. RICKY OSCAR DAHLBERG was born in 1971.

24. **DAKOTA THEODORE SMITH** (Florence Elma Huestis, Frank Revilo Huestis) was born in 1912. He died in 1982. He married GUINEVERE HUNTER. She was born in 1914.

Dakota Theodore Smith and Guinevere Hunter had the following children:

i. WILLIAM JAMES SMITH was born in 1936. He married GLORIA PATTERSON. She was born in 1937.

ii. PHYLLIS YVONNE SMITH was born in 1939. She married FREDERICK SPRENGER. He was born in 1935.

25. **MARVIN REVILO SMITH** (Florence Elma Huestis, Frank Revilo Huestis) was born in 1912. He died in 1962. He married GLADY R. PATRICK. She was born in 1912.

Marvin Revilo Smith and Glady R. Patrick had the following children:

i. MAUREEN ROSE4 SMITH was born in 1934. She married ROBERT DOLAN. He was born in 1929.

ii. RICHARD LEROY SMITH was born in 1939. He married SHIRLEE MURPHY. She was born in 1938.

iii. KAREN ROBERTA SMITH was born in 1943. She married DUANE TAYLOR.

26. DOROTHY FLORENCE SMITH (Florence Elma Huestis, Frank Revilo Huestis) was born in 1914. She married EPHRIAM JUSTIN LEE. He was born in 1901. He died in 1975.

Ephriam Justin Lee and Dorothy Florence Smith had the following children:

    i.   RICHARD JAMES4 LEE was born in 1944. He married (1) JANICE YOUNGINGER. She was born in 1943. He married (2) SYLVIA HOLLAN.

    ii. ROGER GENE LEE was born in 1955. He married (1) PAMELA JEAN MADISON. He married (2) MARY GESTNER.

27. DORA ETTA SMITH (Florence Elma Huestis, Frank Revilo Huestis) was born in 1916. She married HARRY LARS ANDERSON. He was born in 1909. He died in 1989.

Harry Lars Anderson and Dora Etta Smith had the following children:

    i.   AUDREY JEAN ANDERSON was born in 1937. She married RICHARD MOUNTJOY. He was born in 1935.

    ii. RICHARD HARRY ANDERSON was born in 1946. He married DYANN LYNN NELSON FORD. She was born in 1954.

28. HAZEL MAY SMITH (Florence Elma Huestis, Frank Revilo Huestis) was born in 1919. She married MERRILL MURTON ZIMMERMAN.

Merrill Murton Zimmerman and Hazel May Smith had the following children:

i. CHERI JERRINE4 ZIMMERMAN was born in 1948. She married MIKE D. FRAHM. He was born in 1947.

ii. CANDI JO ZIMMERMAN was born in 1949. She married STEVEN E. KREEGER. He was born in 1949.

iii. TAMMI PATRICIA ZIMMERMAN was born in 1957. She married JEFFERY S. HAMILTON. He was born in 1955.

iv. MERILL DEAN ZIMMERMAN was born in 1959. He married PAMELA A. JAQUES. She was born in 1960.

29. **ROBERT ROY SMITH** (Florence Elma Huestis, Frank Revilo Huestis) was born in 1921. He married BETTY ARLENE PEDERSON. She was born in 1924. She died in 1985.

Robert Roy Smith and Betty Arlene Pederson had the following children:

i. GLEN ROBERT4 SMITH was born in 1941. He married (1) MARY BLOODWORTH. He married (2) CINDY BLOODWORTH.

ii. DAVID LEE SMITH was born in 1944. He married LINDA WHITE.

30. **RICHARD ORVAL SMITH** (Florence Elma Huestis, Frank Revilo Huestis) was born in 1925. He married (1) LAURA BURBRIDGE MOSSIER. He married (2) SHIRLEY WHEELER.

Richard Orval Smith and Laura Burbridge Mossier had the following children:

i. SUSAN RALPHINE MOSSIER4 SMITH was born in 1946. She married (1) JIM OSBURN. She married (2) PHILIP JONES.

ii. GRANT RICHARD SMITH was born in 1950. He married KAREN ELIZABETH SKIDMORE. She was born in 1950.

iii. MARK CHRISTOPHER SMITH was born in 1951. He married DIANE RICHARDSON.

iv. BRAD ROLAND SMITH was born in 1955.

31. **VERN IRWIN CRITES** (Achsah Ida Huestis, Frank Revilo Huestis) was born in 1919. He died in 1997. He married ALBERTA MAE STREETER. She was born in 1918.

Vern Irwin Crites and Alberta Mae Streeter had the following children:

i. ALBERTA BETTY4 CRITES was born in 1940. She died in 2003. She married EDWARD CHARLES HAWK.

ii. JACKS ERWIN CRITES was born in 1943. He married LINDA MARIE WOOSLEY. She was born in 1946.

iii. ORIN FRED CRITES was born in 1945. He married PAMELA KAY CHANNELL. She was born in 1950.

32. **CLEONA MARIAN CRITES** (Achsah Ida Huestis, Frank Revilo Huestis) was born in 1921. She died in 1983. She married CARLTON EARL POORE. He was born in 1907. He died in 1984.

Carlton Earl Poore and Cleona Marian Crites had the following children:

i. MARCELLA JEAN4 POORE was born in 1944. She married JAMES JOSEPH EPLER. He was born in 1939.

ii. MERLE CARLTON POORE was born in 1945. He married (1) RITA PETERSON. He married (2) DONNA MALLEY.

iii. DORA MARIE POORE was born in 1953. She married ROBERT JENDRO. He was born in 1950.

iv. LARRY FRED POORE was born in 1955. He married LINDA SPARKS.

33. **DONALD FRANCIS CRITES** (Achsah Ida Huestis, Frank Revilo Huestis) was born in 1922. He died in 1972. He married (1) IONE PANGBORN. She was born in 1918. He married (2) MILDRED PANGBORN BROWN.

Donald Francis Crites and Ione Pangborn had the following child:

i. CAROL DONNA4 CRITES was born in 1943. She married (1) ALTON DAVIDSON. He was born in 1933. She married (2) DALE EDWARD ZENTZIS.

34. **HAROLD HOLLIS CRITES** (Achsah Ida2 Huestis, Frank Revilo1 Huestis) was born in 1923. He died in 2004. He married (1) JOAN ELLENORE MAY. He married (2) OPAL LORRAINE FISHER. She was born in 1924. He married (3) SHEILA M COUTURE. She was born in 1939.

Harold Hollis Crites and Joan Ellenore May had the following children:

i. SANDRA LEE CRITES was born in 1943. She married (1) JOHN SLOAN. She married (2) BUDDY WESTBROOK. He was born in 1941.

ii.	SHERYL LORRAINE CRITES was born in 1946.

Harold Hollis Crites and Opal Lorraine Fisher had the following child:

i.	SANDRA LEE CRITES was born in 1943. She married (1) JOHN SLOAN. She married (2) BUDDY WESTBROOK. He was born in 1941.

35. LOIS LORRAINE CRITES (Achsah Ida Huestis, Frank Revilo Huestis) was born in 1927. She died in 2009. She married LLOYD AMOS OLSON. He was born in 1925.

Lloyd Amos Olson and Lois Lorraine Crites had the following children:

i.	DARLENE GUNDA4 OLSON was born in 1946. She married LARRY TONJUM. He was born in 1944.

ii.	TERRY ROY OLSON was born in 1948. He married (1) MARLA GAIL WILSON. She was born in 1954. He married (2) JANET MOOREHOUSE.

iii.	RHONDA LORRAINE OLSON was born in 1954. She married (1) PETER WILLIAM WORONIK JR.. He was born in 1946. She married (2) ARTHUR PATERA.

iv.	KRISTY LYNN OLSON was born in 1958. She married (1) MICHAEL WILLIAM NELSON. He was born in 1958. She married (2) RALPH PATRICK.

36. DOROTHY JEAN CRITES (Achsah Ida Huestis, Frank Revilo Huestis) was born in 1930. She married ALLAN JAMES KIDD. He was born in 1925. He died in 2005.

Allan James Kidd and Dorothy Jean Crites had the following children:

    i.   LOU4 KIDD was born in 1951. He married KE DANIELSON. She was born in 1958.

    ii. LANA LEE KIDD was born in 1952.

    iii. PAULA JEAN KIDD was born in 1956. She married JIM KEELER. He was born in 1951.

    iv. RENEE ELLAN KIDD was born in 1957. She married TOM BROTHERS. He was born in 1959.

    v. LEE ANN JOY KIDD was born in 1959. She married FRED CHURCH. He was born in 1960.

    vi. TIMOTHY ALLAN KIDD was born in 1967.

    vii. SHELLY LYNN KIDD was born in 1970.

    viii.SHIELA RAE KIDD was born in 1970.

37. DORENE VALARY CRITES (Achsah Ida Huestis, Frank Revilo Huestis) was born in 1931. She died in 2010. She married EUGENE CONARD RUTTER. He was born in 1921. He died in 1995.

Eugene Conard Rutter and Dorene Valary Crites had the following children:

i. CHARLES FREDERICK4 RUTTER was born in 1949. He married (1) KAREN WESSLER. She was born in 1952. He married (2) JENNIFER GREEN.

ii. LARRY GENE RUTTER was born in 1952. He married DEBORHA GENE SHAWVER.

iii. ROGER ALLAN RUTTER was born in 1954. He married DEBORA ANDERSON. She was born in 1954.

iv. WENDY LEE RUTTER was born in 1959.

38. LARENA CRITES (Achsah Ida Huestis, Frank Revilo Huestis) was born in 1932. She married GORDON LYLE STEWART. He was born in 1929. He died in 1998.

Gordon Lyle Stewart and LaRena Crites had the following children:

i. LORNA GAIL4 STEWART was born in 1954. She married CLEMENCE ROY LOCKMAN.

ii. BRUCE ELBERT STEWART was born in 1955.

39. JUNE ARLENE CRITES (Achsah Ida Huestis, Frank Revilo Huestis) was born in 1934. She died in 2009. She married JR. HARRY YOUSO. He was born in 1929.

Jr. Harry Youso and June Arlene Crites had the following children:

i. RONALD DEAN4 YOUSO was born in 1956. He married KAREN KAY WILSON.

ii. MARK WARREN YOUSO was born in 1959.

iii. KIMBERLY ANN YOUSO was born in 1963. She married RICHARD VOISE.

40. JEANNE RAE CRITES (Achsah Ida Huestis, Frank Revilo Huestis) was born in 1942. She married JOE LLOYD JOHNSTON. He was born in 1940.

Joe Lloyd Johnston and Jeanne Rae Crites had the following children:

    i.   DALE CURTIS4 JOHNSTON was born in 1966.

    ii.   DANIEL JOE JOHNSTON was born in 1967.

41. JAMES ALFRED CHVILICEK (Marian Jean Huestis, Frank Revilo Huestis) was born in 1929. He died in 1987. He married CHARLOTTE LORRAINE MEADOWS. She was born in 1930.

James Alfred Chvilicek and Charlotte Lorraine Meadows had the following children:

    i.   JAMES LEONARD4 CHVILICEK was born in 1951. He died in 1987. He married TRACY PHAM THI NHI.

    ii.   LAWRENCE EDWARD CHVILICEK was born in 1952. He married MARY MCLAUGHLIN. She was born in 1955.

    iii. MARIE ANTONETTE CHVILICEK was born in 1954. She married STUART ANDERSON.

    iv. JOHN WILLIAM CHVILICEK was born in 1955.

    v.   PATTY ANN CHVILICEK was born in 1957.

    vi. REBECKA LEA CHVILICEK was born in 1963.

    vii. RAYMOND MATHEW CHVILICEK was born in 1967.

42. **LEONARD GLENRO CHVILICEK** (Marian Jean Huestis, Frank Revilo Huestis) was born in 1930. He died in 1993. He married LOY ANN PATRICK. She was born in 1941.

Leonard Glenro Chvilicek and Loy Ann Patrick had the following children:

    i.   ANNETTE MARIE4 CHVILICEK was born in 1960.

    ii. CHARLES ROBERT CHVILICEK was born in 1962.

    iii. THOMAS LLOYD CHVILICEK was born in 1963.

    iv. JEROME LEONARD CHVILICEK was born in 1964.

    v. STEVEN DOUGLAS CHVILICEK was born in 1966.

    vi. SUZANN LYNN CHVILICEK was born in 1972.

43. **NORBERT FRANCIS ALVIN CHVILICEK** (Marian Jean Huestis, Frank Revilo Huestis) was born in 1932. He died in 1995. He married BERTHA LORRAINE CADY. She was born in 1940.

Norbert Francis Alvin Chvilicek and Bertha Lorraine Cady had the following children:

    i.   SARAH LEA4 CHVILICEK was born in 1960. She married (1) HANS PETERSON. She married (2) JERRY HOAUGEN. She married (3) RICHARD DARLING. He was born in 1966.

    ii. JOEL EDWARD CHVILICEK was born in 1961. He married (1) COLEEN SCHNAKENBERG. He married (2) DAWN LYNN TARBERT.

iii. KENNETH NORBERT CHVILICEK was born in 1964. He married CATHY.

44. LAWRENCE EUGENE CHVILICEK (Marian Jean Huestis, Frank Revilo Huestis) was born in 1934. He married CAROLE ANN STORY. She was born in 1939.

Lawrence Eugene Chvilicek and Carole Ann Story had the following children:

i. PAMELA JO4 CHVILICEK was born in 1962. She married DAVID WILKINS.

ii. JEFFREY PAUL CHVILICEK was born in 1963. He married BRIGID DRISCOLL.

iii. BRADLEY JAMES CHVILICEK was born in 1964. He married MOLLY MCDEVITT.

iv. PATRICIA LYNNE CHVILICEK was born in 1965. She married JEFFREY MACDONALD.

v. MITCHELL PATRICK CHVILICEK was born in 1968.

45. ALICE CAMILLE CHVILICEK (Marian Jean Huestis, Frank Revilo Huestis) was born in 1936. She died in 2005. She married ARNOLD FRANCIS LANGEL. He was born in 1930. He died in 1966.

Arnold Francis Langel and Alice Camille Chvilicek had the following children:

i. EUGENE FRANCIS4 LANGEL was born in 1955. He married LINDA GORDON.

ii. MARRIETTA AGNES LANGEL was born in 1956. She married BARLOW ROALD HAALAND. He was born in 1950.

iii. WILLIAM JAY LANGEL was born in 1958. He married PAT TRIBBY.

iv. JUDY ANN LANGEL was born in 1959.

v. JANET LEA LANGEL was born in 1960. She married PAUL D. TWEDT. He was born in 1959.

vi. DENNIS WAYNE LANGEL was born in 1966. He married DEBBIE LEE RORVIK. She was born in 1957.

46. **ROBERT NOLAN CHVILICEK** (Marian Jean Huestis, Frank Revilo Huestis) was born in 1937. He married BARBARA JEAN OPHUS.

Robert Nolan Chvilicek and Barbara Jean Ophus had the following children:

i. BRIAN ROBERT4 CHVILICEK was born in 1963. He died in 1963.

ii. AMY BETH CHVILICEK was born in 1965.

iii. RITA ELLEN CHVILICEK was born in 1967.

iv. RACHEL JEAN CHVILICEK was born in 1967.

GENERATION 4

47. **MAE EVA JENSEN** (Lucille Mae Smith, Orrie Ethel Huestis, Frank Revilo Huestis) was born on 22 Dec 1946 in Glendive, Montana. She married JIMMIE DAVID RITTAL on 02 Sep 1967

in Circle, McCone, Montana, USA. He was born on 19 Dec 1941 in Circle, Montana.

Jimmie David Rittal and Mae Eva Jensen had the following children:

    i.   KAMI JO5 RITTAL was born on 24 Apr 1969 in Wolf Point, Roosevelt, Montana, USA. She married DOUGLAS ERIC YOST on 05 Jul 2002 in Sidney Rural, Richland, Montana, USA. He was born on 12 May 1971.

    ii.   KALI LYNN RITTAL was born on 04 Jul 1972 in Wolf Point, Roosevelt, Montana, USA. She married PAUL HAKJOONG KIM on 10 Sep 2005. He was born on 19 Jul 1967 in Seoul, Korea.

    iii.   HENRY LUKE RITTAL was born on 06 Aug 1976 in Sidney Rural, Richland, Montana, USA. He married ANN MARIE TOSCANO on 13 Mar 1999. She was born on 09 May 1976 in Danbury, Fairfield, Connecticut, USA.

    iv.   JOHN JIMMIE RITTAL (AKA071216) HANNA VALENTINA PRENTICE was born on 12 Jul 1981 in Sidney Rural, Richland, Montana, USA.

48. TERRY SOREN JENSEN (Lucille Mae Smith, Orrie Ethel Huestis, Frank Revilo1 Huestis) was born on 04 Dec 1948 in Glendive, Dawson, Montana, USA. He married BARBARA ELAINE SUKUT on 17 Dec 1969 in Glendive, Dawson, Montana, USA. She was born on 01 Nov 1949 in Billings, Yellowstone, Montana, USA.

Terry Soren Jensen and Barbara Elaine Sukut had the following children:

    i.   DANIEL ROWLAN was born in 1968 in Helena West, Lewis and Clark, Montana, USA. He married (1) DAWN MICHELLE JONES. She was born in 1968. He married

(2) MANDI MARIE CHRISKE. She was born in 1975. He married (3) SHARLENE ROWLAN. She was born on 14 Apr 1970.

ii. JERRY THOMAS JENSEN was born on 26 Sep 1970 in Billings, Yellowstone, Montana, USA.

iii. TROY SOREN JENSEN was born on 18 Aug 1973 in Circle, McCone, Montana, USA. He married JANELLE LEE CURRY on 13 Sep 1997 in Sidney Rural, Richland, Montana, USA. She was born on 23 Oct 1970 in Miles City, Custer, Montana, USA.

49. DEBRA ANN JENSEN (Lucille Mae Smith, Orrie Ethel Huestis, Frank Revilo Huestis) was born on 29 Nov 1949 in Terry, Prairie, Montana, USA. She married DONALD ALLAN KLEPPELID on 17 Jun 1972 in Circle, McCone, Montana, USA. He was born on 27 Dec 1951 in Circle, McCone, Montana, USA.

Donald Allan Kleppelid and Debra Ann Jensen had the following children:

i. IAN BOSTON KLEPPELID was born on 09 Jun 1982 in Sidney Rural, Richland, Montana, USA. He married KAYLEE CHRISTINE LOVE on 15 Sep 2012 in Huntsville Rural, Walker, Texas, USA. She was born on 21 Jan 1987 in Huntsville Rural, Walker, Texas, USA.

ii. DAMON THOMAS KLEPPELID was born on 16 Dec 1983 in Sidney Rural, Richland, Montana, USA. He married RILEY RENE' CHEATHAM on 02 May 2009 in Shepherd Hill Estates, Willis, TX. She was born on 26 Nov 1983 in Huntsville Rural, Walker, Texas, USA.

50. DAVID THOMAS JENSEN (Lucille Mae Smith, Orrie Ethel Huestis, Frank Revilo Huestis) was born on 06 Mar 1951 in Miles

City, Custer, Montana, USA. He married MARY LYNN GEER on 09 Jun 1973 in Circle, McCone, Montana, USA. She was born on 29 Dec 1955 in Wolf Point, Roosevelt, Montana, USA.

David Thomas Jensen and Mary Lynn Geer had the following children:

i. JOSHUA JON5 JENSEN was born on 18 May 1975 in Wolf Point, Roosevelt, Montana, USA. He married (1) JODEAN WORKMAN. She was born in 1976. He married (2) RENEE LEE MCLEAN on 04 Sep 2014 in Colstrip, Rosebud, Montana, USA. She was born on 11 Feb 1972 in Baltimore, Baltimore, Maryland, USA.

ii. TRACIE ANN JENSEN was born on 27 Aug 1977 in Forsyth, Rosebud, Montana, USA. She married SCOTT HUNTER ROTH on 29 Sep 2001. He was born on 30 Aug 1963 in Rapid City, Pennington, South Dakota, USA

Printed in the United States
By Bookmasters